Called to Transform

ESSAYS ON SPIRITUAL FORMATION IN
CANADA'S CHRISTIAN UNIVERSITY

edited by GORDON CHUTTER

ISBN 978-1-895043-32-7

contents

THE 2,000-YEAR HISTORY OF THE WORLDWIDE CHRISTIAN faith community has witnessed a continual ebb and flow of humanity's response to the grace of God. When there is an ebb, a diminishment of fidelity, a loss of efficacy and commitment, our God does a new thing. He raises up new leadership and creatively acts to bring renewal and revitalization to His grand plan for the world He loves. He does this through His most favored means of grace: human agency. God forms and reforms, designs and redesigns, breathes into and inspires a fresh response to His goodness and grace. In the fullness of time, our Lord works His will for the redemption and restoration of the world, shapes us and gets us in shape for an eternity of fellowship with Him. This is our destiny in Christ, that we work with God, allowing Him to get His hands on the clay of our lives and shape us into the people He intends us to become. We are blessed in God's call upon our lives to participate in this divine work.

The Apostle Paul says it with clarity: "Continue to work out your salvation with fear and trembling, for it is God who is at work in you to will and to do according to His good purpose" (Phil. 2:12, 13, NIV). And what is His good purpose? It is that we be restored to the *Imago Dei*, the image of God. We see the image of God in Christ Jesus, who Paul says was "in very nature God" (Phil. 2:6). Jesus said of Himself, "If you have seen me, you have seen the father" (John 14:9). In short, we are God's project, a project He has been working on for the past 2,000 years leading up to the present and bringing hope for the future. God's hope and plan is that, in the words of the Apostle Peter, we become "partakers of the divine nature" (2 Pet. 1:4). This is God's plan for our total being, our completion in the likeness of Jesus Christ of whom it is written that in His development as a youth He "grew in wisdom, stature, and in favor with God and man" (Lk. 2:52).

Called to Transform is about our complete development in Christ Jesus, about the continuing work of God, in Christ, by the Holy Spirit. It is more specifically about how faculty of a particular kind of academic community—an intentionally Christian university—may come alongside and facilitate the spiritual formation of students in a commitment to whole-person development. It is said that it takes a village to raise a child. In the context of higher education, it takes committed Christian university communities to raise up the next generation of Christ-like leaders to profoundly influence the world and its various marketplaces of life. This book is all about mission fulfillment wherein the University lives out its *raison d'etre*—to develop godly Christian leaders: positive, goal-oriented university graduates with thoroughly Christian minds; growing disciples of Christ who glorify God through fulfilling the Great Commission, serving God and people in the various marketplaces of life.[1]

Ever since the founding of Harvard College in 1636, for 364 years of history in North America, God has been raising-up institutions of higher learning for the purpose of whole-person development in the likeness of Christ. Most institutions

1. The mission statement of Trinity Western University

(e.g. Harvard, Yale, Princeton, Columbia, McGill, McMaster, Brown, Willfrid Laurier, the University of Winnipeg, Syracuse, Dartmouth, the University of Southern California) have lost their first love long ago. They abandoned their first commitment. They no longer encourage faculty to come along-side students and help develop the whole person. They collectively gave up their moral imperative and spiritual mission. *Called to Transform* represents faculty and staff encouraging each other to be instruments of grace in students' lives—to help students fulfill their destinies and be completed in Christ Jesus. May you ponder deeply the insight shared in this book and may you find your response to God's calling in these matters to be pleasing to Him!

Jonathan S. Raymond, Ph.D.
President
TRINITY WESTERN UNIVERSITY

EVERYONE, IN THEIR EVERYDAY WALKING-ABOUT LIFE,
is being spiritually formed. Everything we sense leaves some
imprint on our spirit. The things we see, from grand works
in nature to television commercials, and what we hear, from
words of blessing or worship to scolding disapproval—all these,
and more —leave their mark at the core of our being, our character and personality.

The essence of Trinity Western University is Jesus Christ.
How does He become a living, vital reality in the life of our
academic community? What does it take to have *His* mark left
indelibly on our spirit? Specifically, how is this furthered in
a university setting?

To answer these questions, we must directly and specifically ask, "What roles do Trinity Western University staff and
faculty play in the spiritual formation our students?" This, in
fact, was the question that directed our time together at the
TWU 2009 faculty retreat. Seven presenters spoke to this topic
from their respective areas of interest in classroom teaching, research, and ministry to students.

The idea for the 2009 retreat came from two events during
the 2008-2009 academic year. The first was the 2008 faculty retreat
and its theme of "finding balance: negotiating wellness across

the academic career." This retreat featured guest Jeff Imbach of Soulstream. Jeff's book, *The River Within: Loving God, Living Passionately (206)*, reminds us of our need to know God and His Spirit's empowering in order to live joyful and purposeful lives. Parallel to this event, the 2008-2009 Educational Learning Community (ELC) topic was "spiritual vitality." Through a variety of projects and discussions, the ELC's 18 members, led by Rob Rhea and Vange Thiessen, considered the inward, upward, and outward expressions of spirituality.

Bill Strom, of the Office of Research and Faculty Development, and a member of the 2008-2009 ELC, discerned that the 2009 retreat ought to build on the momentum of the 2008 wellness theme and ELC studies, in a full consideration of "spiritual formation" in our students across the university experience. Speakers were nominated from TWU's Student Life department and from the faculties of Sociology, Nursing, Music, English, and Religious Studies to reflect on this theme. Following the retreat, Jonathan S. Raymond, Ph.D., President of Trinity Western University, urged that these talks be recorded as chapters in a book. The result is *Called to Transform*, a companion volume to the President's *Called to a Higher Purpose*.

In the pages ahead, you will read a diverse collection of writings that speak to one common theme. This is not a tightly written treatise on the subject of Christian spiritual formation; it is a sampler of ideas—a montage written out of the integrity of individual responses to a common question. These chapters are certainly not the last word on this topic, and by no means the only out-working of answers to the question posed to us.

I am so grateful for the work of spiritual transformation that advances, everyday, on the campus of Trinity Western

University. For instance, I know that some faculty and staff gather weekly, under the President's direction, for prayer. Many students attend chapel, every weekday, to worship and to be inspired by top-notch speakers. I know of a member of the custodial staff who has taken the time to listen to students, and who has inspired them by her care and wise counsel. As well, many students attest to the time and effort spent by faculty members in integrating their academic discipline with their Christian faith. Beyond this, some faculty members take the time to listen to the personal needs of their students and to pray with them. And every day, Student Life staff members work tirelessly to minister to students—often serving them without receiving any recognition.

The men and women who serve at Trinity Western University express fidelity to their individual roles on our campuses, and to a higher calling and privilege of working toward our common goal of seeing Jesus Christ formed in the lives of our students. *Called to Transform* lets you in on the thoughts and *praxis* of just a few of our faculty and staff. I know that you will be encouraged.

I wish to thank our authors, Dr. Dirk Büchner, Tim McCarthy, Rob Rhea, Dr. Sheryl Reimer-Kirkham, Dr. David Squires and Dr. Lynn Szabo, who revised their retreat talks to provide the chapters for this book. Rob Rhea has also provided an additional chapter on discipleship and an annotated bibliography for further reading. I am grateful to President Raymond for his transformative leadership of the University and his invitation to create this volume. Several alumni took time to write about their experiences at TWU for which we are thankful. Thanks also to University Communications who took simple documents and crafted the final product.

May the character of Jesus Christ, His words and works continue to be evident in the lives of our students. May God grant faculty and staff at Trinity Western University even greater grace, by His Spirit, to continue this vital work.

- Gordon Chutter

IN MY SECOND YEAR, IN A MOMENT OF RECKLESSNESS, I signed up for a choir audition, and found my name on the list a few days later. After three years in the program, I had a classically trained voice, an outstanding background in choral music, marketable leadership and conducting skills, and the experience of a lifetime. Even more significant, however, was the element of spirituality that was evident whenever we gathered to sing. Dr. Wes Janzen, our choir director, was very deliberate in relating to us the importance of our faith in our music-making. Our performances were immersed in prayer as much as in rehearsal, and we heard many stories from Wes of ways in which people's lives were changed as a result of God's presence in our singing. Since my graduation, I have held many professional positions as an educator and musician in church, school, and community settings, and I have always sought in my work to emulate the principles I learned at TWU both in method and in spirit. However, the greatest ongoing effect of my choral experiences has been not in my career, but in my personal life. In recent years I have lived through some faith-shattering crises, and it is through hearing words of divine truth, expressed in great choral music, that I have been restored.

- Natasha Regehr
BA General Studies 1996, B.Ed. 1997, ARCT (RCM) 2006

WHILE AT TWU I HAD THE PRIVILEGE OF MEETING THREE staff members who began as my coaches, progressed into mentors, and are now my close friends. Alan Alderson (men's soccer head coach) helped me believe in the ability God gave me, not just as a player but also as a leader. Mike Shearon (men's soccer assistant coach) taught me that true success in God's eyes is not found in wins and losses, but in playing for His Glory. Graham Roxburgh (women's soccer head coach) challenged me in my purpose as a player and demonstrated what it was like to use soccer as a platform for fulfilling the Great Commission.

The lessons these three godly men taught over my time at TWU helped turn what looked like the end of my career into a turning point, as I am now a full-time missionary with Athletes in Action while playing professional soccer. An earlier, serious injury caused me to stop, reflect, and prepare for the next chapter of my journey, which was to use my platform as a professional soccer player to share the Gospel. These three men believed in me and I am forever grateful to God for leading me to TWU and for putting them in my life.

- Paul Ballard
BHK Human Kinetics 2006

—

MY TIME AT TWU WAS NOTHING SHORT OF INCREDIBLE. In the four years I attended the University, I can say with certainty that my life was completely transformed. When I entered my first year, I thought I had a good understanding of myself and my faith in God. Nothing could have prepared me for the journey I would embark on. At TWU, I discovered who God created me to be, my gifts, my talents, and especially my passions. I also discovered who I wasn't, and learned to be content and at peace with who God made me to be. My friends, leadership experiences, and professors all contributed to the amazing work that God did in my life during those four years.

- Katrina (Spenser) Henshaw
BA General Studies 2000, B.Ed. 2001

—

THE SUMMER BEFORE ATTENDING TWU, I HAD A LIFE-changing experience on a missions trip to California. For the first time in my life, I could remember truly meeting God and feeling as though He was tangible to me. However, I had a "sinking sand" foundation below my feet without any grounding knowledge of the Bible. My first year at TWU, I took both RELS 101 and RELS 102. Each class gave roots to my faith, which had been based on fire and passion alone. In my last three years at TWU, I learned for the first time what it was like to have godly, Christian friends who support me in my faith no matter how messed up I am. Currently, as a graduate, I look back and see TWU as an experience that not only gave me roots grounding my faith but also gave me wings to explore who God is, and who I am in His eyes."

- Dave Olson
BA Business Administration 2006

—

DURING THESE FOUR YEARS STUDYING AT TRINITY Western University, I have not only gained academic knowledge, but my spiritual life also has been influenced dramatically. When I came to Canada, I learned the basics of Christianity through the Bible. However, as an atheist and an international student, I still found it difficult to understand and accept those abstract concepts until I entered TWU. I have deeply experienced the meaning of love from faculty and staff who cared for both my academic and spiritual life. Different from other universities, Trinity Western focuses on students' spiritual lives. Whenever I meet difficulties, my professors are always willing to help me out. From them, I have experienced God's love and mercy. After four years at TWU, I decided to become a social worker so I can share God's love with others. Now I have graduated, but I will remember what TWU taught me during these years. Trinity Western influenced my spiritual journey and helped me start my new life.

- Helen Huang
BA Sociology 2010

—

THE COMMUNITY AT TWU CHANGED ME! AS I SPENT TIME with peers who were willing to risk everything to follow Jesus, I was challenged. As I enjoyed the loving attention of resident directors and others in the Community Life program, I was encouraged and built up in my faith. As I stepped out to lead and counsel, I was empowered to "sell out" in God's service. One poignant experience I remember happened during my third year at TWU when one of the students from my dorm went to downtown Vancouver to minister to people living on the streets. While riding the Skytrain, she felt a conviction from God that she should approach a stranger on the train to tell him that God loved him and he needed to turn from his wicked ways. I found her boldness outrageous, but I also longed for that kind of confidence in knowing and obeying the voice of God. Her action inspired me to seek God more passionately, and to risk my reputation to follow Him. I have since spent many years seeking to do just that—in Canada, the US, Japan, India, Kenya, and China.

- Kim (Hazelwood) Gilmer
BA Communications 1992

IN MANY WAYS, THE UNIVERSITY EXPERIENCE IS A step into another dimension. The traditional undergraduate's understanding of their identity, the world around them, and life's "big questions" can and should take quantum leaps forward during university. Upon graduation, most students do not look, believe, or think like they did in their first year of studies. University graduates can be a completely transformed version of the person who entered university fours years previously. This transformation is one of the intended outcomes of a liberal arts education with a strong exposure to the humanities. By integrating God's truth with the body of human knowledge and understanding, a liberal arts education fosters critical thought and expands conceptual horizons.

The university, especially the Christian university, must see its role as more than ensuring students complete 122 credit hours. The university must foster a larger vision within their students for God's world and their role in that world. This vision should be big enough to give them a reason to get up in the morning. The idealism, passion, and conviction of university students have changed and continue to change the world in significant ways. For instance, the world missions movement was profoundly affected by a group of university students known as the "Cambridge Seven." As well, the young lives of Jim Elliot, Oswald Chambers, and, more recently, Shane Claiborne have shaped their generations and the generations that have followed. I believe it is a great and high calling to walk with young adults as they move through these years and begin to gain a vision for what their lives can be.

The unique calling of the Christian university, according to the Christian philosopher Arthur Holmes, is not the interaction of faith with learning and culture. Rather, its central calling is the integrative task of critiquing culture and knowledge in light of the truth of God. Implicit in this outcome is the notion that character development and spiritual formation is the *telos* of discursive reasoning and integrative academic rigor. Toward this end, the Christian academy should increasingly orient its students' lives and learning toward the glory of God seen in the classic Christian virtues.

This introduction will explore spiritual formation through initially looking at how spiritual formation is a central task of Trinity Western University as it builds a larger vision of God, the world, and students themselves. It will also look at how the University is a unique context for spiritual growth and will address some of the background, implications, and core facets of the term "spiritual formation." The bulk of the section will be a practical exploration of how formation can be developed within the three dynamics of the inward life, the outward life, and the upward life.

Spiritual Formation Defined

The notion that the believer's life should increasingly become more like that of Christ is nothing new. Jesus called His followers to deny themselves, take up their cross and follow Him

(Lk. 9:23). Paul called the faithful to be conformed to the image of Christ (Rom. 8:29). And Peter challenges Christians to be holy as God is holy (1 Pet. 1:15-16). These challenges have resulted in the general theological category known as sanctification. Through the years, alternative terms such as "spiritual theology," "Christian spirituality," and, in this case, "spiritual formation" have come into more common usage to, in part, bring focus to a neglected dimension of this broader theological category. Regardless of the terms used, it should be recognized that these terms collectively refer to the important task of the exploration of the nature and dynamics of growth in Christian holiness.

Spiritual formation is not a Protestant, Orthodox, or Catholic term; it is an ecumenical, Christian term. Spiritual formation could generally be defined as the process of forming the believer, through the agency of the Holy Spirit, so that the essential dimensions of the believer's life become like that of Jesus. There can be little argument that this is at the heart of authentic Christianity. Formation should lead to a balanced approach of the initiating work of God in our lives and the antiphonal response of our own efforts. In *Letters by a Modern Mystic*, Frank Laubach wonderfully captures this in saying that the individual's role is to open the windows—that God will do all the rest. Spiritual formation builds within the Christian the ability to do the right things for the right reasons.

Sanctification or spiritual formation is described in many ways throughout the New Testament. The transformation of the human heart into the likeness of Jesus is described as taking off the old self and putting on the new (Eph. 4:22-24), growing up into Christ (Eph. 4:15), and abiding in Christ (Jn. 15:5). All of these images speak to a thorough ongoing renewal of all aspects

3

of the human heart. It is, as the *New Living Translation* renders Ephesians 3:17, Christ making His home in your heart as you trust Him. Sanctification or spiritual formation is at the core of the mission of TWU, and is expressed in both the essence and ends of the University. One of the stated core educational outcomes of the University is spiritual formation as seen as striving for TWU students to be persons who "learn to love God, to embody a Christ-like and Spirit-empowered way of life, and to be characterized by their selfless love for and service to others" (Wood, 2008). Reframed under more generic headings, formation can be conceived as being supported through three dynamics or dimensions: the inward life, the outward life, and the upward life. Together they form a balanced approach to growth in the wisdom and knowledge of God.

Inward Life

It has been said that the inward journey is the longest journey you will ever take. The journey a soul takes as it is formed into an increasing likeness of Jesus Christ is epic in its scope. The heart and mind of one who has walked with God for a lifetime is a masterpiece of grace and transforming love. While there are many important facets of the transformed inner life, two stand out as particularly important for university students: identity in Christ and the practice of spiritual habits or disciplines to become like Christ and help others become like Christ.

Identity is central in the life of a university student. The university is a context where students are continually evaluated. Their intelligence is assessed through graded assignments. Their social desirability is reflected in the ability or lack of ability to achieve a vibrant dating life. For athletes, their status on the team is marked by the number of minutes played, points scored, or finish times recorded. In the wake of these success markers, a student's identity can be constantly up for grabs. An important theological issue for university students is knowing one's identity in Christ. Therefore, an essential educational outcome of Christian higher education must be moving students to realize that enduring significance comes only from God. The scriptures speak beautifully to this truth.

> Therefore, there is now no condemnation for those who are in Christ Jesus. (Rom. 8:1, NIV)

> There is no fear in love. But perfect love drives out fear. (1 Jn. 4:18)

> You are God's chosen people, holy and dearly loved. (Col. 3:12)

> You are a chosen race, a royal priesthood, a people for God. (1 Pet. 2:9)

> You are more than conquerors through Christ who loves us. (Rom. 8:37)

The theological lexicon of the Christian university student must be filled with the truth that nothing the Christian student will ever do or not do can separate them from the love of God.

In my experience, if you ask the typical university student how someone grows in their faith, the answer is almost always the same: spiritual disciplines. Activities such as prayer, reading the Bible, and journaling, just to name a few, are recognized as essential to growth. 1 Tim. 4:7 says, "Discipline yourselves for the sake of godliness." The important step for university students to make is engaging the disciplines as a means and not an end in themselves. The practices or activities of forming a deep Christian faith is a life-long quest and is especially difficult in our culture of instant gratification. Superficiality is the tone of a broader culture. Our culture is filled with image without substance, wealth without work, pleasure without principles, and the list goes on. The spiritual disciplines connect and slow our souls. They connect our earthly lives with something bigger and eternally significant. In *Renewing Your Spiritual Passion* (1997), Gordon MacDonald recounts the story of an African explorer who was relentlessly pushing his expedition through the bush. One morning he could not get his native helpers to shoulder their loads and begin walking. When he asked why they were not moving, they replied that they needed to "let their souls catch up to their bodies" (P. 24). In more than a few ways, the disciplines allow room for our souls to catch up with our bodies. If students can learn to take time away to spend time with their Father as Jesus did, then they are positioned to face the challenges of the world of adulthood.

The disciplines provide a sort of "training wheels" for our hearts and minds to be progressively transformed into the likeness of Jesus. Two areas of particular challenge for university students are scripture reading and observing the Sabbath. Regular exposure and meditation on the truths of scripture and prayer provide university students with perspective and grounding in the midst of radical changes and over-commitment. When students are exhausted, discouraged, and feel like they are losing sight of who they are, the words "come unto me all who are weary and heavy laden and I will give you rest" (Matt 11:28) are the perfect invitation.

One of the most challenging yet desperately needed disciplines is regularly observing the Sabbath. With university students, there are few commodities more precious than time, but the commandment to remember and keep the Sabbath holy is a point where "the rubber meets the road" in a student's willingness to trust God for their academic success. Moreover, the Sabbath provides one of the most concrete opportunities for students to see God's faithfulness in the reality of their lives.

Outward

If the Christian life was comprised entirely of the closed loop of the believer's communion with God, there would be no need to go further than the inward life. In reading the Bible, though, it becomes readily apparent that the reach of a relationship with God has implications that extend beyond the self to the rest of humanity. The great commandment says that after loving God with all that is within us, we are to love our neighbour as ourselves (Mt. 22:37-39). In large part, the measure of spiritual maturity is seen in the quality and consistency of our relationships. Relationships with those in authority, with the opposite sex, with the poor and oppressed, just to name a few, are of central importance to the message of Jesus. If TWU is to be fully successful, its graduates should be redemptive influences in their relationships and respective contexts.

Few things are more important to today's university students than their friendships. The ubiquitous presence of texting, status updating, and social networking websites are a testament to students' need to stay connected. *The New York Times* reported that in 2009, 75 per cent of American teens had cells phones, and that the average teenage girl sent/received 2,272 texts per month (nearly 80 per day) with teen boys sending/receiving 30 texts per day. If nothing else, it is clear that students value ongoing and unabated contact.

Relating well with the opposite sex is as much of a challenge within the church as it is outside the church. Notre Dame scholar, Christian Smith, a leading researcher of the 18-23 year old demographic, shows in *Souls in Transition* (2009) that 35 per cent of the most devoted, non-married Christians in this demographic have experienced sexual intercourse (P. 275). If one includes those who identify as less devoted but still regular attendees (two to three times per month), the number grows to 67 per cent. If these statistics describe the experience of TWU students to any degree, TWU must provide an informed and compelling voice for the freedom that can be found in embracing God's design for relationships. Repeated exposure to God's truths regarding sexuality and family must be a priority in Christ-centred education. Through giving the larger picture of God's design for relationships, sexual ethics flow out from the right source, thereby avoiding legalistic or puritanical reasons for action.

Another characteristic of a TWU education is the emphasis on dimensions of ethical leadership. Students' faith convictions should motivate them to be redemptive change agents in the broader culture. In *Faith Works* (2001), Jim Wallis, the Washington, D.C., based social reformer and activist says, "the greatest heresy of the 20th century is that faith should be a private matter" (P. XXVII). A full understanding and embracing of the gospel must move the Christian toward addressing the needs of the world around us. Wallis goes on to say that poverty has three faces: material, spiritual, and civic. Material poverty is the form of poverty that first comes to mind. The scriptures are replete with God's supreme interest in the plight of the poor.

As Proverbs says, "He who shows contempt for the poor mocks their creator" (14:31). Spiritual poverty occurs when the heart and internal motivation for doing good are absent. The heart is the primary focus of God (1 Sam. 16:7; 2 Chr. 16:9) and is the beginning point for needs to be met over the long haul, for the right reasons. Civic poverty occurs when citizens abandon their responsibility to provide and care for the marginalized and vulnerable. Vital to authentic Christian faith is the concern for these. As Jesus states in Matthew 25:40, what we have done for the "least of these in this world," we have done for Him.

Upward

A life that is focused on "the things above, where Christ is" (Col. 3:1) will be increasingly characterized by an attitude of worship and a growth in godly wisdom. One of the great quests in the life of a Christian student, and the Christian life in general, is bringing worship out of Sunday mornings and connecting it to the whole of our lives. Our segmented lives enable a false mindset of worship being relegated to a particular time and place. While there must be a dedicated time and place for the body of Christ to gather, the activity cannot be pigeonholed. The goal is to bring an ongoing communion with Christ into all areas of our lives: education, relationships, work, and ministry. This lifestyle of worship maintains a Trinitarian focus: to God, through Christ, by the agency of the Holy Spirit. As we strive to maintain our focus on God, our lives will begin to reflect the glory of God with ever-increasing measure, and will be characterized by spiritual wisdom and insight. True spiritual wisdom will shape the priorities that govern our lives and promote right action.

As Richard Foster states in *Celebration of Discipline* (1988), "to worship is to experience Reality, to touch Life" (P. 158). In worship, we respond to what we know and have seen to be true about the glory and character of God. William Temple, in *Hope of a New World* (1997), beautifully captured this in saying:

> *In worship, we quicken our conscience by the holiness of God, feed our mind with the truth of God, purge our imaginations with the beauty of God, open our hearts to the love of God, and devote our will to the purposes of God.* (P. 30)

Worship is an all-encompassing activity that shapes and informs how God has revealed Himself throughout history and specifically in the person of Jesus Christ. In worship, all of Christ's offices, such as Teacher, Guide, Redeemer, and King, are brought into full focus and view.

In the life of a university student, worship has a central and stabilizing influence. As mentioned previously, students face many challenges to their identities. If they are doing well in their classes or are socially fulfilled, they can feel secure in their self-worth. If these or other circumstances are not the case, then self-condemnation can ensue. One of the first and best influences of worship on our lives is the recalibration that it brings. We are reminded that our only hope for fulfilment and acceptance is found solely in the fact that a good God loves us unconditionally, what Robert McGee (1990) refers to as "enduring significance." The hubris that so often exists on a university campus is shown for what it really is in light of the holiness of God. Humility has been defined as thinking rightly of oneself and is a cardinal virtue in the practice of worship. Worship brings us to a point of restful humility in light of the sufficient love of God.

Godly wisdom is a natural consequence of a vibrant life of worship and a mature understanding of our identity before God. Christian education, or any education for that matter, that does not see growth in wisdom as its goal is short-sighted and lacking. Wisdom could be said to be skill in living, seeing life in light of God's larger purposes. This is what the psalmist refers to in saying, "Teach us O Lord to number our days aright that we may gain a heart of wisdom" (Ps. 90:12). John Calvin (trans. 2008), in the opening sentence of his *Institutes of the Christian Religion* captures this in saying, "Nearly all the wisdom we possess, that is to say, true and sound wisdom, consists of two parts: the knowledge of God and of ourselves" (p. 4).

Derek Kidner, in his commentary *Proverbs* (1981), proposes that Proverbs acts as prism, breaking wisdom into its many constituent parts for closer consideration. In his discussion, he develops the notion that wisdom has a dynamic quality as it guides, instructs, and informs the mind. It brings change to the heart and guides the decisions. It is something that is hard-won, yet is a gift from God (Prov. 2:6). Wisdom contrasts the ways of the wisdom of God as being a "tree of life" (3:18) versus the way that seems right, but whose end is death (14:12). Wisdom distinguishes the maturing Christian and should be a central focus of Christian higher education.

Conclusion

In *The Fabric of Faithfulness* (2006), Steven Garber has articulated three primary influences that set a trajectory of spiritual growth beyond graduation day: a matureing worldview, role models that embody what students aspire to become, and like-minded peers who are committed to similar goals. Trinity Western is uniquely gifted and resourced to strongly contribute to these three central influences. Through our interdisciplinary courses and integrative commitments, the construction of a Christian worldview is one (perhaps the strongest) commitment we aspire toward as an institution. Through faculty, staff, and off-campus guests, students are repeatedly exposed to role models that embody the character and wisdom that we are attempting to instill in our students. Our campus residence policy (all students except those who live at home must live on campus until they are 21 or have third-year status) and strong student leadership program make our commitment to peer interaction and mentoring clear. As students develop peer relationships that value the same commitments to truth and the kingdom of God, they will be well positioned as they move from TWU into their chosen spheres of influence. As Trinity Western can work to provide and establish these factors in the lives of their students, our graduates will have the vision and skills to make a real difference in the world.

In the following chapters, members of the TWU community consider the broader issue of spiritual formation from their unique perspective. The perspectives are from both faculty and staff, reflecting the multi-faceted nature of spiritual formation within the academy. In the first chapter, Gordon Chutter reflects on the centrality of 'person,' not only in the helping professions, but in the classroom and in ministry to students. How we present ourselves to others is a key factor in shaping their lives. Recognizing the biblical pattern that it is disciples who make disciples, he argues that who we are as disciples of Jesus Christ—in our own personal journey—is *most* significant in shaping the spiritual lives of our students.

Dr. Sheryl Reimer-Kirkham is a leader in nursing education and expresses her passion to teach in a way that informs spiritual formation in her students, and through them, substantively changes the lives of their patients. In Chapter Two, she elaborates on the aim of the School of Nursing to provide education that encompasses transformation, holism, covenantal caring, and social justice.

Dr. Dirk Büchner shares, in Chapter Three, from his own journey on the teaching of religion in light of the broader task of spiritual formation. As an Old Testament scholar and teacher, he wants to be faithful to the task of developing sound thinking about the text, in ways that serve to inform and form students' faith journeys. This balance is achieved when instructors show care for their students as people and as learners, while applying academic rigour to classroom discussion and allowing freedom of expression.

In Chapter Four, Rob Rhea argues that the process of Christian spiritual formation is inextricably tied to the biblical notion of 'disciple.' He shows that being a disciple of Jesus Christ has definite implications for both belief and behaviour. Making disciples of Jesus Christ implies, therefore, that we engage in *certain* tasks towards *specific* outcomes or ends. It is the clarity about the meaning of 'disciple' that drives the means and methods that we choose.

Next, Tim McCarthy moves from a consideration of disciple-making in the broad context of revelation, to specific methods of discipleship, including faculty and staff engagement in corporate worship, and in counseling, practicising hospitality and praying with students. This chapter issues a call to faculty and staff to model a life of faith that students can emulate.

In Chapter Six, Dr. David Squires draws on his years as a teacher of musical composition, relating his passion to see music crafted as an expression of the *Imago Dei*—the creativity of

God. Musical composition is far more that mastering technical complexity. Music is an expression of the heart and this, he argues, needs to be valued, affirmed, and evoked in our students.

In the Afterword, Dr. Lynn Szabo draws together the themes of our 2009 faculty retreat. She shares our deep desire to see Christ formed in the lives of the people who are part of the community known as Trinity Western University, and to see evidence of this spiritual formation expressed inwardly, outwardly, and upwardly.

-Rob Rhea

REFERENCES

Calvin, J. (*trans.* 2008). *Institutes of the christian religion.*
Peabody, MA: Hendrickson

Claibourne, S. (2006). *The irresistible revolution.* Grand Rapids:
Zondervan.

Elliot, E. (1970). *Through gates of splendor.* Grand Rapids:
Revell.

Foster, R. (1988). *Celebration of discipline.* San Francisco:
Harper.

Garber, S. (1996). *The fabric of faithfulness.* Downers Grove:
Intervarsity Press.

Holmes, A. (1983). *All truth is God's truth.* Downers Grove, IL:
Intervarsity.

Kidner, D. (1981). *Proverbs: an introduction and commentary.*
Downers Grove: Intervarsity.

Laubach, F. (2007). *Letter by a modern mystic.* Colorado
Springs: Purposeful Design Publications.

MacDonald, G. (1997). *Renewing your spiritual passion.*
Nashville: Thomas Nelson.

McGee, R. (1990). *The search for significance.* Houston, TX:
Rapha Publishing.

Smith, C. (2009). *Souls in transition.* New York: Oxford Press.

Temple, W. (1941). *Hope of a new world.* New York: Kessinger.

Wallis, J. (2001). *Faith Works.* New York: Random House.

Wood, R. (2008). *Curriculum review task force: A summary
report for the undergraduate academic council of Trinity
Western University.* Langley, BC: Trinity Western
University, Office of the Provost.

Gordon Chutter, MA, MAL, is a sessional Assistant Professor of Sociology and Practicum Coordinator for the Human Services Certificate program. The Certificate program equips students who are considering a career in the helping professions by introducing them to the values, attitudes and praxis skills associated with high-quality professional care. His particular interest is in the spirituality of care.

chapter 1

Discipleship in Human Services

GORDON CHUTTER

The Context of Much of Western Christianity

I ONCE HEARD ABOUT A MARRIAGE THERAPIST WHO WAS meeting with a couple that had a *very* boring relationship. In an effort to spark this relationship, he asked this couple a question. "What is one thing you would like your spouse to do for you that would *really* improve your marriage?" After few moments, the husband replied, "I know what I *really* want from my wife... it's clean socks!" We laugh, or weep, at the husband's response, because we know that what could have been a multi-layered, rich, vibrant transformative experience, for both husband and wife, is reduced by his comment to a minimalist transaction. The man settled for less, and he was content to do so.

At this retreat, we are exploring a topic that is pressing us to engage more deeply with students, with one another, and with God, than perhaps we wish to. It's pushing our 'marriage' to another level.

Our partnership with Jesus Christ calls for us to pursue Him with all our heart, and mind, and soul. This is the mark of a disciple. Much of what we do here at Trinity Western University is parallel to what transpires in many of our local churches. We must exercise vigilance in our union with Christ, and in the way that we model it to succeeding generations.

Dallas Willard contends that, "So far as the visible Christian institutions of our day are concerned, discipleship is clearly optional" (2006, P. 4). He goes on to say that "one is not required to be, or [required to] intend to be, a disciple in order to become a Christian, and one may remain a Christian without any signs of progress toward discipleship" (P. 4).

Perhaps in the churches we attend, it is sufficient that we become Christians without making a lifelong commitment to continuous transformation as disciples of Jesus Christ. We show up, we pay up, we contribute some act of service, and we are counted as 'in.' We put in time, energy and money; and in exchange, we get respect and possibly membership. It's a transactional arrangement that is not necessarily spiritually transformative.[1] It's a tidy ecology—a conspiracy between leaders and led. Our leaders (pastors and priests) expect no more, and neither do those whom they lead. We've settled for less in some of our churches—why on earth would we settle for more on the campus of a Christian university?

And because we come out of this church ethos, it may be enough that we are knowledgeable in our fields, enough that we are reasonable as communicators and administrators, and

1. The distinction between transactional and transformation leadership is attributed to Burns, James McGregor (1978) *Leadership*. New York: Harper and Row, and more fully articulated in Ford, Leighton (1991) *Transforming Leadership - Jesus' Way of Creating Vision, Shaping Values & Empowering Change*. Downers Grove: Intervarsity Press.

enough that we are cordial to our peers and students. If we meet this minimum threshold, we are counted as members in good standing of the community of TWU. We have the loyalty of those we lead (because we help them achieve their academic and professional goals), and in exchange we get paid and promoted. We expect nothing more of ourselves, and students are not beating down our doors asking, "I want to be a disciple of Jesus—will you teach me?" Like the church, our campus community is also a very tidy ecology/conspiracy.

Emulating Jesus? Loving one other sacrificially? Embracing the Beatitudes as a guide to life and living? Only keeners need apply. So if we are to engage as disciple-makers, we are not simply tweaking church and campus policy. We are engaging in effecting a *paradigm shift* in the way our faith is conceptualized and lived out, in both church and campus life.

Definition

Each of this year's retreat speakers was asked to supply a definition of spiritual formation.

Dallas Willard says that spiritual formation in the Christian tradition is "a process of increasingly being possessed and permeated by [certain] character traits as we walk in the easy yoke of discipleship with Jesus our teacher. From the inward in character deeds of love then naturally—but supernaturally—and transparently flow… Our aim is to be pervasively possessed by Jesus through constant companionship with him" (2006, P. 16). "We are meant to be inhabited by God and to live by a power beyond ourselves" (P. 26). For Willard, "Christian spiritual formation is the redemptive process of forming the inner human world so that it takes on the character of the inner being of Christ himself" (P. 105).

In other words, Christian spiritual formation is a gradual,

pervasive infusion of Christ's character and mission into the lives of ordinary people. The key word is *infusion*. My metaphor is that this process is like the infusion of tea in a cup of hot water. After a few moments, we rename that 'cup of hot water,' a 'cup of tea.' There can be no greater compliment paid to a Christian than to say he or she is thoroughly infused with the character and zeal of Jesus Christ.

Disciples, then, are these ordinary folks who are *extraordinarily* infused. Mostly this is due to God's work, and some of it has to do with desire and disciplines of those being infused.

Our Context

Let me say a few words about how this works out in our discipline. I teach some of the Sociology courses at Trinity Western University, and I also teach the core courses in the Human Services Certificate Program. The certificate is a 30-semester-hour program embedded in the degrees of Sociology, Psychology or Social Sciences. Here, we help students to *apply* the knowledge gained across the undergrad curriculum, especially the social sciences, as it relates to helping people. Some of our students head directly to work in probation services, group homes, street youth work, etc. Others, after graduating from TWU, pursue advanced degrees in counselling psychology, social work, and addictions counselling. The Human Services Certificate Program affords our students a great opportunity for spiritual expression and formation.

In our curriculum, we address three domains of enquiry: context, process, and self.

Regarding the *context* of care, we cover:
- a summary of the history of the provision of care through the

church and state
- a sociology of care: who gets it and who is excluded
- social policy in Canada, history of policy, and policy making
- professional ethics and legal aspects of caring

Under *process,* we address:
- a paradigm of persons (how we view the nature of person)
- models of care
- strategies of intervention

Under *self,* we discuss:
- self-care, burnout, and personal wellness
- time management; rest and sabbath
- spirituality of care
- the use of a learning journal
- vocational discernment

A very important component of our program is the completion of three practicum placements totaling 300 hours of service in social services agencies and ministries. These experiences afford our students opportunity for personal and professional development, vocational discernment, as well as spiritual formation. In the marketplace, they begin to apply the lessons taught in the classroom. Henry Fielding once wrote, "Adversity is the trial of principle, without it, a man hardly knows whether he is honest or not." Many of our students, after completing a practicum, would say that Fielding was right.

There is one theme that emerges again and again in practicum seminar; it is the notion of 'self as agent.' Of all our assets, capacities, and gifts, our *lead* strength is our person, our self and the way we present ourselves to others. The core of our self is our character. In our *Introduction to Human Services* class, I relate a story about the time when I was eleven years old and suffered what turned out to be appendicitis. My mother called our family physician, a man by the name of Dr. Grimson. I still remember this older, kind, gentleman coming upstairs to my bedroom carrying his well-worn black bag—a symbol of his profession and seasoned expertise. What impressed me was not his professional competence—although this proved to be essential in the operation that ensued the next day—but it was his kindly presence. The point I make with our students is that our personality, and especially our spirituality, are not a subtext in our encounters with others. They are what we lead with. In the task of helping others, it is not the stuff in our 'black bag' that impresses our clients (or in our case, our students). It is not our credentials, nor is it our technique that are the primary means of transformation. Establishing rapport and empathy are vital to the therapeutic process, and they are key to all relationships that are transformative.

Individuals are not to be primarily viewed as an object of concern, but as subjects of an encounter—an encounter that changes both the giver and the receiver. Competent, caring professionals move away from 'it : it' relationships and move towards 'I : thou' (person to person) relationships. We are to view persons as sacred, made in the image of God. We are to pray, 'Thy Kingdom come; Thy will be done on earth as it is in Heaven' and we are to work relationally to usher in a kingdom of right relations. I want our Human Services graduates to be person-centered, not simply clinically-focused.

Hidden Curriculum

It is on this point of 'self as agent' and 'I : thou' relationships, I am most self-conscious. I am cognizant of the need to model what I teach. I am aware that students are watching me and my interaction with them. They are students of the course content, and also they are students of me (and all of us). There is a hidden curriculum in every lesson that I teach.

In every interaction with every student, I am engaging in spiritual formation/discipleship. The question is, who or what am I discipling them unto? (I may be the closest that any of them has come to the Gospel, to Jesus.)

This leads us back to our retreat theme: "What roles do TWU faculty play in the spiritual formation and discipleship of our students?"

As one who teaches sociology, the word 'roles' is a bit of a red flag. May I digress here for a few moments to teach you some terms as they are used in sociology? In explaining how we understand what guides our social interaction in everyday life, sociologists tell us that we relate to one another according to our statuses. These include our gender, race and ethnic origin, and the socio-economic status that we are born into. Statuses also include our martial status, our sexual orientation, our present socio-economic status, and other factors that define us as persons. A simple definition is: status is a social position that one holds, gains, or loses. A set of statuses evolves over the course of life and statuses re-pattern much like the elements in a kaleidoscope. We label ourselves and we label others according to our statuses. Knowing the statuses of others helps us know how to relate to them and guides our everyday social interactions with them.

Some statuses are more important to us than others. Sociologists use the term 'master status', for a status that has special importance in shaping social identity. In the presentation of self in everyday life, we are careful to manage image and present our package of statuses in such way that is advantageous to us at any given moment. Now back to the word 'roles.' Roles, sociologists tell us, are the behaviours expected of someone who holds a particular status.

With these definitions in mind, we could rework the question that is guiding our retreat. "What roles do TWU faculty [in their status as faculty] play in the spiritual formation/discipleship of our students?"

Here's another question: "What roles do TWU faculty [in their status as disciples of Jesus Christ] play in the spiritual formation/discipleship of our students?"

I find this to be a far more searching question because it causes me to ask whether I have ever identified myself as a disciple of Jesus. I am more likely to see my faith as something that colours, informs, influences my other statuses. Am I a disciple of Jesus Christ? Is that a status that defines me? Is it my master status?

Here's why this is important. The Biblical pattern is that *disciples make disciples.* Disciple-making is one of the roles of the particular status called 'disciple of Jesus Christ.' If am to disciple others unto Christ, with integrity, then I must declare myself as a disciple of Christ. We still haven't addressed the question of 'what roles?' Since we live out of our hearts, it may be more instructive to look at our hearts as disciples.

Our students have come to Trinity Western University for many reasons. Some of them want to mature into Christ-likeness. Imagine a student who wants to be discipled. They might wish to interview you, to see whether you are, in fact, a disciple of Jesus Christ. (Please note that all of us are constantly verifying statuses, in order to determine whether our expectation of a role behaviour is a reasonable expectation.)

Here are some questions that might be fair game:

1. "Do you really believe this stuff—these Christian propositions?" (You answer, "Yes I do, in fact I have signed a declaration to that effect as a condition of employment... I also try to integrate faith principles with my academic study." They might press us further: "Do you live your life as though this stuff is true?")

2. "Who is Jesus to you? I know you're a disciple of your discipline. Are you a disciple of Jesus? I mean, is your relationship with Jesus Christ the foundation of everything else in your life?" (Read: 'master status.')

3. "How close are you to Jesus? In John's gospel, Jesus urges His disciples to remain in Him (Jn 15:4) and to remain in His love (Jn 15:9). The writer of Acts notes in 4:13 that Peter and John were men who had been with Jesus. So I want to know, what is the emotional quality of your friendship with Jesus right now?"

4. "How do you grow in your closeness to Jesus? How do you hit the refresh button so that you remain in Jesus? How do you maintain your in-loveness with Jesus? Do you employ spiritual disciplines? Which disciplines have you found to be effective?"

5. "What's your motivation? I see lots of performance-oriented people—students, faculty and staff. Do you get caught up in all that posturing? I once read that James Dobson believes that we spend our adult lives meeting the unmet needs of our childhood. So what is your motivation? Do you do what you do to get love (recognition and applause), or more so to express the love that you have received?"

6. "What issues are currently facing your walk with Jesus Christ? For instance, are you seeking His face above seeking His hand of blessing? Here's another one: if Jesus is the 'Alpha male' have you surrendered to Him?"

7. "The last thing I want to know is, do you care about me? Do I matter as a person to you? Do you care about my growth as a person?"

The roles we assume are important. They are a means to an end—they express our statuses. I invite us to articulate and strengthen a particular status in our lives: disciple of Jesus Christ. The means (or roles) flow from an intention to see a particular end realized. May we have the grace to image ourselves as His disciples—disciples who just happen to work at a university. May we be led to creative roles to express the essence of that status. May we lead out of our person, not the 'black bag' of our professional disciplines.

Each academic year, there are students who come to Trinity Western University who are seeking a transformative encounter with Jesus, mediated by caring peers, faculty, and staff. They are looking for more than the 'clean socks' of a simple transactional exchange. May we be found faithful in representing the person of Jesus Christ in all we say and do. By God's grace, may we be part of many spiritually transformed lives—disciples, abiding in Him, who set our hearts on discipling others.

REFERENCES

Burns, J. M. (1978). *Leadership.* New York: Harper and Row.

Ford, L. (1991). *Transforming leadership – Jesus' way of creating vision, shaping values & empowering change.* Downers Grove IL: Intervarsity.

Willard, D. (2006). *The great omission – Reclaiming Jesus' essential teachings on discipleship.* New York: Harper Collins Publishers.

Sheryl Reimer Kirkham, RN, Ph.D., is Associate Professor in the School of Nursing at Trinity Western University, where she is Director of the Masters of Science in Nursing (MSN) program and teaches health care ethics, health policy, and qualitative research. Her scholarship focuses on diversity and social justice in healthcare and nursing education. A current funded research project examines religion, spirituality, culture, and place in home health care. Sheryl is a founding member of TWU's Religion in Canada Institute and Institute of Gender Studies, and has recently been awarded a 2010 Award of Excellence in Nursing Research by the College of Registered Nurses of British Columbia (CRNBC). She has authored numerous peer-reviewed manuscripts, and her dissertation was awarded the Governor General's Gold Medal at University of British Columbia. Sheryl lives in Surrey, B.C., with her husband and two daughters.

chapter 2

Spiritual Formation & Social Justice in Nursing Education:
Seeking an inspired integrated approach

SHERYL REIMER-KIRKHAM

SPIRITUAL FORMATION HAS MANY DIMENSIONS AND expressions, both inward and outward. Gladson (2004), a pastor and professor who writes about spiritual formation in relation to social justice, asks how to balance, on the one hand, spiritual formation with emphasis on the individual, spiritual direction and the shaping of spiritual life, and on the other hand, the ministry of social justice with its stress on the community. The inward spiritual life and social justice are mutually constitutive; the inward spiritual life sustains outward expressions of social justice, and compassionate acts that further social justice likewise feed the internal life. Acknowledging the foundation of a rooted, life-giving internal spiritual life, in this chapter I focus on the second half of the dialectic between inward and outward spiritual formation, individual and community—that of social justice.

Social justice is a recent "growth industry" receiving increasing attention in academic circles and community sites alike, across faith-based[1] and secular contexts. What is not as common is an emphasis on the inextricable ties between spiritual formation and social justice. My interest here is in exploring how higher education within the Christian tradition[2] fosters spiritual formation as inclusive of social justice. Engaging in a conversation about spiritual formation in higher education, inevitably, has one speaking from the vantage point not only of one's faith perspective, but also of one's discipline—even as we strive toward interdisciplinary perspectives. My particular entrée into the dialogue is through the profession of nursing, speaking from my position as Associate Professor of Nursing. After some introductory comments about spiritual formation and social justice, I draw on examples from our experience and research on student learning in community practica (what we refer to as "clinical placements") to bring focus to questions such as: "What role do professors have in spiritual formation?" and "How might we engage students in service as a 'means of grace' toward spiritual formation?"

Our mission at TWU, a Christian university, is distinctive. While teaching the substance of nursing in order that our students graduate as competent nursing professionals, we also strive to contribute to the process of spiritual formation so that graduates are transformed. Do I overstate our uniqueness? Higher education has a tradition of concern with moral and spiritual

---

1. There is recent debate among some circles about whether an emphasis on "social justice" takes one toward or away from the heart of the Christian faith tradition. The interpretation of social justice in this paper draws on the numerous Biblical injunctions to care for the poor, alien, and needy with compassion; to "love mercy, do justice, and walk humbly with our God" (Mic 6:9, NIV). With colleagues, I have written elsewhere about the importance of social justice perspectives to nursing (Reimer Kirkham & Browne, 2006; Anderson et al., 2009).

formation, and nursing education in particular has a long history of wedding professional and moral development. Contemporary nursing curricula have integrated program ends that include moral statements regarding social justice, often using the language of moral development. Indeed, with spirituality a popular pursuit and a hot topic in society, there is now a breaking of the silence in the academy about the role of spirituality in higher education (Tisdell, 2007; Hooks, 1994), sometimes under umbrella terms such as "transformative education," "reflective learning," "experiential and participatory pedagogy, intuitive and imaginative processes, and contemplative practices" (Duerr, Zajonc, & Dana, 2003). Exemplifying this trend is the following introduction to a paper entitled "In the New Millennium: The Role of Spirituality and the Cultural Imagination in Dealing with Diversity and Equity in the Higher Education Classroom" by Elizabeth Tisdell (2007) at Pennsylvania State University: "…it is time for a new approach to critical multicultural teaching in higher education, to one that emphasizes social justice, an end to oppression, and spirituality…" (p. 531). While there is this renewed interest in the spiritual in higher education, I suggest that the degree to which we seek spiritual formation here at TWU, and the specific vision of this formation as participating in God's divine intent for humankind, is distinct. I lay the groundwork to support this argument with exploration

---

2. I see the relationship between spiritual formation and social justice as taking particular forms in different religious and secular traditions. We have argued (Pesut et al., 2009) that rather than proceeding in a supposed generic interpretation of spirituality (spiritual formation in this case), it is more useful to particularize or situate explorations of topics such as spiritual formation and social justice within specific faith traditions. This chapter is written from my location as a Christian within a Mennonite tradition, teaching at Trinity Western University, an evangelical Christian university.

of the definitional nature of both spiritual formation and social justice.

Considering Spiritual Formation and Social Justice

The invitation to address the faculty on the topic of spiritual formation and social justice gave me pause to think about spiritual
formation and the related terms of *in*formation, *re*formation,
and being formed, *con*formed and *trans*formed into the image
of Jesus Christ. What variation of formation are we interested in?
A couple of anchoring points provide shape to the discussion.

> 1. From Scripture, we have the encouragement to "grow
> in the grace and knowledge of our Lord and Saviour
> Jesus Christ" (II Pet. 3:18, NIV). Spiritual formation
> involves a process of increasing in grace and knowl-
> edge in a relationship with Christ.
>
> 2. Spiritual formation is the process of being conformed
> to the image of Christ by the gracious working of God's
> spirit, for the transformation of the world. Individual
> growth is the route to something beyond us!

Richard Foster (2003) makes the observation that our goal as
Christians is not heaven (though that is our final destination)
but rather to have Christ formed in us. He also notes that we lack a
theology of this growth—we need to learn how we cooperate with
"the means of grace" that God has ordained for the transformation of the human personality. Foster categorizes the means of
grace for spiritual formation as follows:

> EXPERIENTIAL MEANS · God works first through
> the ordinary experiences of daily life to form the char-

acter of Christ in us. Experiential means include work viewed as sacrament, trials that produce endurance, and movings of the Spirit.

FORMAL MEANS · The formal means of grace refer to well-recognized disciplines of the spiritual life such as prayer, fasting, solitude, simplicity, confession, service, and celebration.

INSTRUMENTAL MEANS · Instrumental means are various means of grace (human and physical), again widely recognized, through and with which God transforms us. The scriptures and the Lord's Supper are two examples.

Foster suggests that disciples of Jesus Christ *cooperate* with these means of grace to be changed into Christlikeness. From these anchoring points in regard to spiritual formation, we can gather that: (1) clearly, spiritual formation as a concern of a professor is quite different than imparting and facilitating acquisition of information; (2) we are part of a much larger process—spiritual formation (**trans**formation) in the hearts of students does not depend on us, but we can be part of the process. We can **create conditions** that foster soul transformation; and (3) spiritual formation is for large purposes, including a close relationship with Jesus, but spiritual formation is about more than piety—spiritual formation is about transformation of the world toward God's ends.

How do we understand social justice in the context of spiritual formation? Again, several anchoring points are offered. Quoting scripture from Micah: "He has told you, O mortal, what is good;

and what does the Lord require of you but to do justice and to love kindness, and to walk humbly with your God" (6:8 NRSV). The starting point of scripture reminds us that oppression and injustices are unfortunate realities around us: "If you see the poor oppressed in a district, and justice and rights denied, do not be surprised at such things" (Eccl. 5:8, NIV). Scripture has numerous references to poverty, and it is my conviction that our students need guidance in being freed from our North American social blinders (e.g., values of individualism, wealth, consumerism) in a reading of scripture, in order to hear God's heart for justice, His compassion for the poor, and His anger at injustice.

We engage students around social justice in recognizing how social position structures life opportunity and how certain people carry the social burden of illness. Several examples demonstrate the social nature of suffering, and what is called for by social justice. The HIV/AIDS epidemic to Africa has a profound global social unfairness to it. Closer to home, Aboriginal women are at high risk for HIV/AIDS, complicated by historical and ongoing colonizing processes, poverty, and violence (McCall, Browne & Reimer-Kirkham, 2009). A further example of the structural nature of suffering is that of the results of the deinstitutionalization of the mentally ill that occurred in the 1980s and 90s. Without proper community supports, many among the most vulnerable in our society ended up in a cycle of criminalization, between homelessness and incarceration (Lamb & Weinberger, 2005). Each of these examples point to justice requiring both redistribution and recognition because injustice has both economic and cultural dimensions (Fraser, 2003).

We have seen repeatedly that as students become informed of the root causes of these types of injustice, they tend to become engaged in efforts toward individual and social transformation. They recognize they are part of a larger divine process. Social justice as a moral end (ideal) is accomplished in an eternal sense. As professor, I participate in a historical global epic narrative when I seek to foster students' commitment to social justice. While we share concerns for spiritual formation and social justice with secular institutions of higher learning, our participation in the cause takes its moral imperative and inspiration from the Christian scriptures.

Spiritual Formation and Social Justice in Nursing Education

In this section, I draw on some examples from our efforts in the School of Nursing to bring together institutional mission, curriculum, experiential learning, and research—all for the joint cause of spiritual formation and social justice. Coherence between the institutional mission and curriculum has been important; the curricular philosophy for the School of Nursing reiterates the institutional mission at several levels. We have seen a beautiful unfolding as students learn in a culture where questions about social justice resonate across campus, classroom, and clinical practice experiences. Four curricular values—transformation, holism, covenantal caring, and social justice—are posted on banners in the School of Nursing.

TWU Nursing is:

transformation ~ holism ~ covenantal caring ~ social justice

TRANSFORMATION
change in character, impact on culture

HOLISM
shalom, integrating physical, psychological, spiritual,
social, and environmental dimensions

COVENANTAL CARING
sacred commitment, inestimable value of humans,
response to human suffering

SOCIAL JUSTICE
inclusivity, dignity, and opportunity for health; moral
mandate to attend to marginalization and inequities

More than dry words, these concepts are integrated into nursing courses as students learn about the social determinants of health that include education, employment, food security, housing, income, and social exclusion (Raphael, 2009). Students study the conditions and effects of poverty, considering for example what it means to live in a province (British Columbia) with the lowest minimum wage — one that has not increased in ten years — and where more people than ever have only part-time work.

Added to institutional mission, curricular philosophy, and course content, are experiential opportunities (clinical practica) in settings where students come face to face with health and social disparities. Such settings for student learning include correctional facilities, aboriginal communities, international placements, and mental health facilities. Recently, nineteen students travelled to Zambia with two nursing professors to learn firsthand about global health, community development, and the ravages of HIV/AIDS in Africa. Over the years, such international experiences have raised questions that have prompted deep consideration in the realm of spiritual formation and social justice for students and faculty alike. It was this dissonance that prompted several nursing professors at TWU to engage in a research project with nursing students.

International travel studies, as part of the internationalization of education, are becoming increasingly popular as claims about transformative learning are made. Yet, surprisingly little is known about the long-term effects of these placements. The literature focuses predominantly on short-term learning (reporting on learning during the experience with little or no follow-up). This gap is exacerbated by the focus on benefits for the North American students who travel rather than the experience for host communities. To address this gap in a beginning way, we conducted a two-year project entitled "Keeping the Vision Following International Learning Experiences"[3] (for details of the project please see: Reimer-Kirkham, Van Hofwegen, & Pankratz, 2009). The purpose of this participatory action study was to explore the nature of learning about Christian perspectives of social justice in the context of international health experiences, and to support students in integrating this learning into personal and professional domains when they return to Canada. Over the period of a year after students returned from their international placements, three professors engaged intentionally with students through discussion groups, specific projects (e.g., fund-raising for villagers in Guatemala devastated by mudslides, an HIV/AIDS fundraising walkathon), and communication (a bulletin board and email newsletter) to keep social justice initiatives in the forefront.

3. We are grateful for funding for this project from the Social Sciences and Humanities Research Council of Canada, Aid to Small Universities Program.

Study findings revealed that while students reported profound learning from their international experiences, it was difficult for them to sustain the enthusiasm and to integrate learning into home settings (Reimer-Kirkham et al., 2009). Students repeatedly remarked that seeing firsthand the lived realities of poverty, lack of housing, and malnutrition brought home to them the social determinants of health as much more than a theoretical concept. This is powerfully reflected in the following participant comment: "statistics... become faces of people I know." This comment brings into focus the importance of not only learning about social determinants of health, but doing so in relationship with those living in impoverished circumstances, as these relationships became powerful vehicles that allowed students to see people not as the disadvantaged "other" but rather as fellow human beings. "People are the same everywhere." Yet, significant intentionality was required for ongoing engagement in issues of social justice to make the international learning experiences part of a coherent educational program, rather than a one-off or a "bubble on the ocean of life," as one student described the four-week international placement. Another student observed: "it's very easy to come back here and forget what it's like down there. You get on with life." Based on the study, we drafted a preliminary set of recommendations for international experiences (Reimer-Kirkham et al, 2009) that focus on maximizing transformative learning for the long run, fostering equitable partnerships, and generating more knowledge about international travel studies. In the context of short-term missions, several Christian scholars have begun some groundbreaking work to address similar concerns (e.g., Friesen, 2004; Ver Beek, 2005).

Based on our experience and research, non-traditional

clinical placements and experiential learning can be instrumental in spiritual formation and social justice. Yet, the intentionality required is not to be underestimated, nor the risks of perpetuating historical and continuing colonizing relations. Where the aims of spiritual formation and social justice have been *integrated* across institutional mission, curricular philosophy, and learning experiences, the university community together works to create the conditions to serve as the means of grace for spiritual formation. Undoubtedly, these efforts must be *inspired* by the Holy Spirit.

Concluding Questions

In conclusion, I return to the questions I raised earlier: "What role do professors have in spiritual formation?" and "How might we engage students in service as a 'means of grace' toward spiritual formation?" My stance is that my primary obligation is that of teaching students to become competent professional nurses, and, in the process, I participate in creating conditions that may become means of grace toward spiritual formation. I invite continued dialogue on these questions—they are not questions with ready answers. I am tremendously humbled and encouraged to be engaging in such questions with committed colleagues. When the role of professors in facilitating spiritual formation in the dimension of social justice is understood as cooperating with means of grace, we quickly recognize ourselves as co-pilgrims with students in this journey of spiritual formation, seeking higher ends — Kingdom ends.

REFERENCES

Anderson, J., Khan, K., Peltonen, A., Rodney, P., Varcoe, C.,
    Browne, A., Reimer-Kirkham, S., Lynam, J., McDonald,
    H., Tan, E., Wong, S., Baumbusch, J., Semeniuk, P. (2009).
    Inequities in health and health care viewed through the
    ethical lens of critical social justice: Contextual knowledge
    for the global priorities ahead. *Advances in Nursing Science.*
    32(4), 1-13.

Duerr, M., Zajonc, A., & Dana, D. (2003). Survey of
    transformative and spiritual dimensions of higher education.
    Journal of Transformative Education, 1(3), 177-211.

Fraser N. (2003). Redistribution or recognition? A critique
    of justice truncated. In: Fraser N, Honneth A, eds.
    *Redistribution or recognition? A political philosophical
    exchange* (P. 9-25). London: Vorso.

Friesen, R. (2004). *The impact of short term missions on beliefs,
    attitudes, and behaviours of young adults.* Unpublished
    doctoral dissertation. University of South Africa. Available at:
    http://etd.unisa.ac.za/ETD-db/theses/available/etd-07222005-
    083203/unrestricted/thesis.pdf

Foster, R. (spring 2003). Becoming like Christ. *Knowing & Doing.*
    Accessed August 20, 2009 from: http://www.cslewisinstitute.
    org/files/webfm/knowing_doing/BecomingLikeChrist.pdf

Gladson, J. (2004). Spiritual direction in the social justice
    tradition. In G. Moon and D. Benner (eds.) *Spiritual direction
    and the care of souls: A guide to Christian approaches* (PP. 137-
    151). Downers Grove: InterVarsity Press.

Hooks, B. (1994). *Teaching to transgress: Education as the practice of freedom*. New York: Routledge.

Lamb, H., & Weinberger, L. (2005). The shift of psychiatric inpatient care from hospitals to jails and prisons. *Journal of the American Academy of Psychiatry Law*, 33(4), 529-534.

McCall, J., Browne, A., Reimer Kirkham, S., & Spittal, P. (2009). Struggling to survive: The difficult reality of Aboriginal women living with HIV/AIDS in an urban context. *Qualitative Health Research*. 19(12), 1769-1782.

Pesut, B., Fowler, M., Reimer-Kirkham, S., Johnson Taylor, E., & Sawatzky, R. (2009). Particularizing spirituality in points of tension: Enriching the discourse. *Nursing Inquiry*. 16: 337-346.

Raphael, D. (Ed.) (2009). *Social determinants of health* (2nd ed.). Toronto, ON: Canadian Scholars Press.

Reimer-Kirkham, S. & Browne, A. (2006). Toward a critical theoretical interpretation of social justice discourses in nursing. *Advances in Nursing Science*, 29(4), 324-339.

Reimer-Kirkham, S., Van Hofwegen, L., & Pankratz, D. (2009). "Keeping the vision": Sustaining social consciousness following international learning experiences. *International Journal of Nursing Education Scholarship*. 6(1), article 3.

Tisdell, E. (2007). In the new millennium: The role of spirituality and the cultural imagination in dealing with diversity and equity in the higher education classroom. *Teachers College Record*. 109(3), 531-560.

Ver Beek, K.A. (2005). *The impact of short-term missions: A case study of house construction in Honduras after Hurricane Mitch*. Final Report. Calvin College, Grand Rapids, Michigan.

Dirk Büchner, D.Litt., teaches Hebrew and Old Testament in the Department of Religious Studies. His main research emphasis is in Septuagint studies, and on the more popular level, the dialogue between the Bible and science.

chapter 3

Some Remarks About Spiritual Formation & Academic Integrity

DIRK BÜCHNER

THIS ARTICLE IS THE RESULT OF MY REFLECTIONS ON a book called *Teaching and Learning in College Introductory Religion Courses*, by Barbara Walvoord (2008).

This past December, I reached a 20-year milestone in teaching large Old Testament Intro classes. During the first decade of my teaching career, my students were Zulu-speaking Africans and English-speaking East Indians who had some faith background and a deep love for the Bible. Some of them, however, were suspicious of the Bible because of its misuse by those who planned and implemented Apartheid in the decades between 1948 and 1990. But because the Bible was precious to them, they and I could make wonderful discoveries together through our interaction on topics such as the Bible and land ownership, the Bible and politics, conflict and reconciliation. They discovered that the Bible was their book and that their own readings were valid. My time of learning with them was a very fruitful one.

I have just completed my ninth year at TWU and have taught

an Old Testament Intro class since 2002. This time period has been no less fruitful. TWU students from Canada and the US have a similarly strong faith background but come with a confidence in the Bible as fully integrated with their culture, which brings with it its own set of challenges.

Barbara Walvoord opens her book by asking: "What do we know about the spiritual expectations of American college students?" She quotes a recent survey done by the Higher Education Research Institute at UCLA, which found:

> Today's college students have very high levels of spiritual interest and involvement. Many are actively engaged in a spiritual quest and in exploring the meaning and purpose of life. They are also very engaged and involved in religion, reporting considerable commitment to their religious beliefs and practices. As they begin college, freshmen have high expectations for the role their institutions will play in their emotional and spiritual development. They place great value on their college enhancing their self-understanding, helping them develop personal values, and encouraging their expression of spirituality. (2008, P. 24)

In view of this, Walvoord asks very early in her study what goals students have for taking classes in religion. Alongside these goals she compares goals that faculty have for the students taking their religion courses. By this she approaches the business of goals from both ends. Her study of dozens of classes finds that across the board, student goals are: acquiring of factual information or a body of knowledge, and developing their own personal moral and ethical values.

On the other hand, faculty goals are, without exception: getting students to become critical thinkers and analysts.

By critical thinking, we faculty understand things like: being habitually inquisitive, well-informed, trustful of reason, being open-minded, honest in facing personal biases, and being clear about issues and orderly in complex matters.

I found helpful Walvoord's presentation of the way that Belenky et. al. describe the acquisition of critical thinking as a set of moves:

- from *silence*, in which one has no voice or cannot be heard,
- to *received knowing*, in which one relies on external sources for truth, (church, peers, authority figures)
- to *subjective knowing*, in which the self asserts its opinions but resists reference to external sources or tools,
- toward *procedural knowing* which includes mastery of academic tools that are part of analysis and critical thinking and are manipulated without the investment of the self,
- and finally towards *constructed knowledge*, an adult position where the self and the tools are integrated. (1968, P. 65)

When we compare the goals between students and faculty, there appears to be a gap, or what Walvoord calls "the great divide" between student goals and faculty goals.

Having identified this gap, Walvoord goes a step further to draw a comparison between public universities and religiously affiliated institutions. She found that faculty at both types of institution prized learning to analyze and critically evaluate as the top goal for their students, while they placed developing values in fourth position. There was a difference in the case of the students. Students at public universities ranked developing values third while at religious institutions it was ranked at the top.

I think that we need to reflect on what that means for faculty and students at TWU. I am not sure whether it is good news or bad news.

For Walvoord, there is a complex web of causes underlying students' preference first for knowledge acquisition and then developing values. She suggests that among them are the fact-focused orientation of students' previous schooling, their culture's strong emphasis on faith as an individual emotional experience, and their culture's suspicion of the academy. Many students come ready to learn but also ready and prepared to resist any challenges presented to them.

My intention in presenting this data is not for us to debate the problem without attending to some solutions. Walvoord gives most space in her book to careful case studies of what she calls "highly successful faculty" who wrestle with the great divide and come up with creative solutions. There is no single cure-all, but successful faculty typically achieve the integration of analytical thinking with students' personal spiritual development by:

1. Having clear goals and conducting continuous conversation with students about goals throughout their courses

2. Constantly examining their pedagogical strategy

3. Caring for students and taking seriously their goals

Successful pedagogy creates spaces and voices by which students can integrate critical thinking with their own spiritual growth. A crucial element in the achievement of this seems to be discussion. Students throughout the research wanted more discussion if their courses were to improve. What is meant by creating spaces and voices? Faculty create spaces where students feel safe from ridicule or from fear that questioning is wrong. Good spaces are also those where plenty of discussion takes place, both in small and large groups, both student-led and faculty-led.

Faculty create voices for articulating beliefs where students become analysts, informants and formulators of arguments. Faculty create voices in which students learn to become listeners and seekers. Not invited in this atmosphere are the bigot or the dutiful, compliant student who treats the class merely as an exercise to be completed.

It may be noted that though students valued discussion more than just about anything else, the faculty registered their frustration at not being able to generate as much discussion from the students as they had hoped.

Spiritual Formation and Critical Thinking

In my course I find it hard *not* to achieve a goal of spiritual formation. Year by year I find that I can let the material do its work of challenging the students about spiritual formation, with little prompting from my side. This was indeed the finding of many faculty participating in Walvoord's study. Students are very good at aligning course material with their need for personal development. But a challenge for me is to integrate spiritual formation with critical reflection. Armed with the knowledge that the gap is bridged when faculty are seen to care for their students, when their goals are carefully articulated, when students are given frequent opportunities for discussion, and when faculty get the students to ask "why" questions, I try to be more intentional about these things.

Let me provide an example of how I go about my goal of integrating critical thinking with acquisition of values, on the assumption that spiritual formation happens when both of these come into play.

My course has a discussion component of one hour per week for every student, in smaller groups. How well discussion groups go depends on a number of factors. Group A on Monday will talk up a storm whereas Group B on Wednesday will be stone dead. Next week the opposite may be true. But in any case, I try to get them to do some reflection beforehand. Here are two typical passages I would assign the students for study and discussion:

The first is the Eden narrative in which Adam and Eve meet the snake. There is a serious interpretive problem that we have to face in this story. God said that if the humans were to eat the forbidden fruit, they would die on the very day that they ate. The snake said that this was not true. Now, any reader would expect that when God says something will happen, it *will* happen. Instead, it turns out that the snake's reading of the consequences is presented to the reader as the correct one. The disobedient humans carried on living. The snake therefore appears to have 'got it right.' More than this, these are God's very first words to the humans. If these words somehow turn out to be untrustworthy, the natural question we ask is this: Can God be trusted when He warns about the results of disobedience? Why would God back up His prohibition with a threat of death if He meant something different? We can think of what happened to well-meaning Uzza in 2 Samuel 6:7, or to devious Ananias and Sapphira in Acts 5.

This is not all. God does not supply the "because" line, such as: "You will die *because* that is a poisonous fruit," or "*because* you'll know too much for your own good". It is the snake that supplies the "because" line and it is a very negative one: God knows that He can keep you un-seeing by this prohibition. And this is the kind of thing you can expect of God—His commands are designed to inhibit you rather than to grant you freedom. Besides supplying this restrictive "because" line, the snake turns the consequences of the act into something attractive: you won't die but will become all-seeing, like gods. He doesn't suggest what Eve should do but he creates the space for her to do it, and she responds to her inclinations.

So, in this foundational narrative, both God's truthfulness and His trustworthiness are called into question. It also happens in a problematic way, because it is like a parent giving a child a stern warning which is contradicted by a shifty, unreliable character, whose opinion is justified by the way things turn out. The child is unlikely to take the parent's warnings seriously from that time on.[1]

Reflection on this can go in various directions:

1. A THEOLOGICAL READING

The text reveals that people get away with disobedience. The expected consequences weren't apparent to the perpetrators however much this may be apparent to us, the readers, who understand a more metaphorical meaning for "die." The text reveals that God's fair judgement does not always come in ways we expect.

On a constructive level, the text leads the reader to anticipate that there are, and will be more, credible and reliable voices in our lives that will entice us to call into question that God is trustworthy and whether He should be obeyed at all. This puts before us the age-old challenge to acquire a reasoned faith: do we abandon

1. This example is taken from Moberly, R.W. L. 2008, pp. 22-40.

faith in a God who is good, when our experience tells us the opposite or when we have the motive and opportunity to do so? Or do we dig deeper into faith and find better foundations for belief in God and obedience to His commands even when more logically attractive options are available?

For some students, there was no problem to be recognized in the text. God simply meant that humans would on that day cease being immortal and become mortal. That solution appears to settle the matter and remove all difficulties of interpretation. To this one could respond that there is nothing in the Genesis narrative to indicate that man was created immortal or that eating from the tree of knowledge had anything to do with changing that status. If that were true, the snake would surely have got some mileage from it. For him, the act of eating would instead lead to becoming like God, meaning knowing good from evil (not living forever). For him it was about their eyes being opened, and that is the concern of the text, not immortality. It was interesting for me as an instructor to observe how difficult it was for some students to recognize that there was any wrestling to be done with this text before it could be appreciated.

2. A HISTORICAL READING

This text also offers me the opportunity to show students that we need to learn how to read Biblical texts historically. This narrative is what may be called a sacred telling or sacred tableau with a moral lesson. I say this because for comparison there are countless pictorial representations from Israel's surrounding cultures that date from the period when the Bible was being written, of sacred tableaus containing among other things, people and animals in relation to gods. Most commonly a tree would be found in the centre of such pictures. These tableaus had a similar function to the Eden narrative: they belong to a special kind of symbolic telling that uses representative figures: —an animal, a human, a snake, a tree. These symbols express significant aspects of the artist's sacred world, and he or she achieves meaning by *participating* in that symbolism. From the gathering of much evidence we have come to know that the tree had in the early Iron Age (when the Israelites emerged) become the replacement symbol for the goddess figure. In the Fertile Crescent, the goddess' role was to bring fertility in plants and animals, and her universal presence among Israel's neighbours, trading partners, and political allies, was always a source of temptation and stumbling for God's people. Those who first received the Eden narrative would no doubt have recognized in it the goddess symbolism, long before they asked any other questions of the story. We have to take that seriously. God revealed the Bible to appeal to those ancient Middle Eastern hearers and readers. They had a sensitivity for the symbolic, unlike us with our modern curiosities and sensibilities. We have to be honest and ask why the narrative contained that particular subject material. A strongly plausible reason is that the Eden narrative wanted to express sin's presence and effect in the world of humans, by means of a sacred story that resonated with other, familiar sacred tellings, though these contained a goddess. The Bible's account dethroned the goddess but retained some of the attractive aspects of the tree. The first readers could participate in the symbolism of the story far better than we are able to and we need to try to stand in their shoes if we are to fully appreciate the Bible's significance.

By this I wish to illustrate that there is more to the Eden narrative than what is probably traditionally treated in an introduction course. What I try to do is get the students to recognize two things. One is that the text itself has a voice and wants to confront at the same time their need to acquire spiritual acumen and their sense of reason. The second thing, and equally important, is to recognize that the text has an ancient context which has to be known and studied before we can come to a full understanding of what it can communicate.

There is another set of Biblical texts that invite our sense of critical reflection because of the way in which they have been taken "at face value" in the past, as regular sources of factual information. These are the texts from Deuteronomy and Joshua to do with the conquest of Canaan. In them, God demands military violence in the name of cleaning out wicked nations from His good land. We all know that the Canaanites were wicked enough for the land to vomit them out (Lev. 18:28), and if the goal was for God's people to survive, morally, the obliteration of women and children (Deut. 20:14) appears to present us with no difficulty. That conclusion removes the need for further reflection on the material. Every year I hear students coming up with this simple solution that settles the issue and renders it unproblematical. Some textbooks lay the matter to rest in similar fashion.

1. A SOCIO-POLITICAL READING

But perhaps you are someone who grew up in a setting where, in recent memory, land had been taken from others by violence. Or perhaps you have had the opportunity to listen to the way the victims of land-grabbing, or their children, read those same Bible texts. If so, you would be forced to take a critical look at the way the Bible has been read and understood by success-oriented or dominant cultures (in my case, it meant taking a critical look at my own culture). You may perhaps also have done some reading about the subject of 'the Bible and ideology' and realize that you don't have to look very hard to find in the relationship between Deuteronomy's instructions and Joshua's conquest an analogy for the way the Bible has been co-opted, in an 'off the page,' literalistic reading to support the imperialist model in Western history. God had a covenant with some group and their task was to rid of evil some territory into which they were migrating, whose inhabitants then became their enemies.

This was the way Cromwell viewed divine legitimation for his invasion of Ireland in the 1650s, and the way in which early migrating South Africans in the 1830s viewed their victory over the Zulus as God-given—to name but two. In the modern context, this idea often lay behind the "just war" motif in recent history. We can add a note here that the Living Bible, a document of 1960s American culture, calls the Biblical Philistines "Palestinians!" A perfect example is how Jewish settlers in the West Bank and Gaza defy the international rule of law by appeal to the Bible. Then again, if you are someone who has felt the effects of ethnic cleansing a little closer to the bone than the average Christian living in conflict-free surroundings[2], the mere association of these texts with genocide may raise difficulties that you would have to work through very carefully.

(This is not to deny the way in which 'off-the-page' liberationist readings of the book of Exodus have served to support the understanding that God required the blanket overthrow of colonialist governments and was in total support of whatever was perpetrated by liberation movements in Latin America and Africa, for example. The dire economic consequences of Africa's

2. And I think we all can, by simply reading of events in Rwanda, Armenia, Algeria, Kosovo, or Kurdistan.

and Latin America's revolutionary and post-colonial intellectual basis, will now have to be documented and analyzed in the light of Biblical interpretation.)

2. A HISTORICAL READING

There is again an ancient cultural aspect that partially accounts for Israel's God being portrayed in warlike terms. If He weren't, then those who first heard about Him might have preferred not to believe in Him. We know that the lawgiving in Deuteronomy contains very similar terminology to the treaties made between the ancient Hittite rulers and their subjects. Typical of these kinds of agreements, threats against unfaithfulness far outweigh the merits of obedience (See Deut. 28). Israel would not have been content with something phrased in more reasonable terms, such as a modern software 'user agreement.' It stands to reason that when Yahweh appears in the Bible as a military victor against Egyptians, Canaanites, and the forces of nature, He was expected by its first readers to come with all the accessories of other warrior deities familiar to them. It so happens that precisely at this time, two deities appear prominently in the sacred artwork of surrounding cultures, with particularly warlike characteristics. They are the Egyptian Reshef and the Canaanite Baal, both of whom are portrayed in action, bearing weapons of war above their heads, ready to strike. Reshef is not without his spear, and neither is Baal without his club.

From what we know of the pervading worldview, any enemies of a person's nation are also the enemies of that person's God, which makes them enemies worthy of total annihilation. To suppose otherwise would have been unthinkable at the time. When Achan kept for himself a few valuables after the sack of Jericho, what he really did was break the rules of the cosmic order itself, whose repercussions were beyond his imagination.

By drawing students' attention to these kinds of questions, I hope to get them to read these texts, ready to do some deeper reflection. So, in their midterm exam, they are required to answer the following fairly open-ended question:

> *Respond to the accusation that Deuteronomy's view of conquest, as carried out by Joshua, has provided religious support for much of the land-grabbing and brutality witnessed in, for example, Cromwell's actions in Ireland, western colonialism in Africa, North America and South America (not to mention Israel's occupation of the Palestinians' land).*

As a guide to responding, I suggest to the students that we Western Christians have to acknowledge that the Bible has been, and can still be, read and applied incorrectly by us. This offers us an opportunity to make things right. It offers us a challenge to learn how to prevent similar mistakes in the future, especially in cross-cultural settings such as ours. Compare the questions following the chapter on Joshua, from popular textbooks with an evangelical focus:

A. Describe the three major waves of Joshua's campaigns.

B. How does the book of Joshua convey the possession of the land as an act of worship?

C. Do you think Joshua was successful in fulfilling God's plan for his life?

I would argue that these types of questions relate only to the students' desire for knowledge acquisition and spiritual growth. They are not intentional in fostering any kind of critical reflection. If, on the other hand, successful pedagogy creates the opportunity by which students can integrate critical thinking with their own spiritual growth, and creates the opportunity for students to integrate the self and the academic tools available to them, I hope that through my work I am striving ever harder to take students in further directions that befit an academic Christian institution.

What I have shown in this chapter is that the questions we ask push classroom discourse in particular directions. In our religious studies classes, I want to honour our students' desire for spiritual growth, while fostering a pedagogy that drives students to think critically. For the sake of their spiritual growth, I try to create an atmosphere where students are invited to think deeply about the meaning of the scriptures they read. It is this deeper engagement with the text that allows students to consider how the text might be applied in, for example, an analysis of the assumptions that informed and directed certain historical events, or the assumptions that guide contemporary culture. This understanding and application fosters a more mature engagement with God, the Word, and our world—a mark of a growing disciple of Christ.

REFERENCES

Belenky, M. F., Clinchy, B. M., Goldberger, N. R., & Tarrule, J. M. (1986). *Women's ways of knowing*. New York: John Wiley.

Moberly, R. W. L. (2008). Did the interpreters get it right? In *Journal of Theological Studies* 59 Oxford: Oxford University Press.

Walvoord, B. (2008). *Teaching and learning in college introductory religion courses*. Malden, IA: Blackwell Publishing.

Rob Rhea is the Chaplain and Director of Student Ministries at Trinity Western, a position he has held for 14 years. He is a Ph.D. candidate at Talbot School of Theology and serves as the Director of TWU's Centre For Spiritual Formation In Higher Education.

chapter 4

THE MANY FACETS OF BEING A DISCIPLE OF JESUS CHRIST

ROB RHEA

FROM HIS CALL TO "COME AND FOLLOW ME" TO THE current moment, Jesus calls men and women to follow Him and to be His disciples. In this same vein, Jesus calls university students to follow Him in deeper ways, and He uses Christian universities to assist in the disciple-making endeavor. This chapter takes an extended look at the biblical background and meaning of the term disciple. Next, it explores three essential dimensions of being a disciple and stages people pass through as they become more committed disciples of Jesus within the biblical narrative. Insights into what it means to follow Jesus are provided in the metaphors of the soldier, athlete, and farmer found in II Timothy. The final portion of this chapter examines practical issues surrounding the disciple-making process for university students.

One of the central focuses of Trinity Western's mission statement is the commitment to develop "growing disciples of Jesus Christ." This declaration sets TWU apart from most institutions of higher education and has brought a considerable amount of critique. The broader Canadian academy often sees this commitment as inherently limiting; compromising true expression of academic freedom. A commitment to Christ, they might say, necessarily limits the pursuit of truth. A disciple of Jesus is caricatured as narrow, provincial, and simplistic. All of this discussion raises the question, "What actually is a disciple of Jesus Christ?" It is essential that our institution have a clear understanding of this key biblical concept as we develop our curriculum and respond to those outside the community. Though the word 'disciple' has been worn smooth through our repeated use, its implications are gripping and reach the whole of who we are as individuals.

Disciple is a weighty term in the New Testament. The call to follow Jesus and be His disciple does not come without a price. In Paul's conversion on the Damascus road, Ananias is told that Paul will be shown how much he must suffer for God's name (Acts 9:16). As Paul nears the end of his life, he minces no words in articulating what the faithful life will require. The Christian will be able to remain faithful in challenging circumstances only through being strengthened by God to "be strong in the grace that is in Christ Jesus" (II Tim. 2:1 NIV). We are saved solely by the grace of God, and we live each subsequent day solely through the grace of God. It is by this grace that we will be able and willing to endure the suffering and hardship associated with following Jesus. We can rest assured that He is worth the sacrifice and that the reward of the faithful life will be of immeasurable worth.

This chapter initially investigates how the notion of "disciple" has been used within the Bible as a theological term. The focus then specifically turns to II Timothy 2:1-7 to explore the passage's unique framing of what being a disciple of Jesus entails. The result will hopefully be a richer understanding of what it means to follow Jesus and how that can be lived out in the families, churches, and ministries of which we are a part.

Survey of Discipleship

USE IN THE OLD TESTAMENT

Though the term disciple in the Old Testament is rarely used, the notions of teaching and learning are present. Within the OT, the idea of spiritual relationship appears most often within the context of covenant, particularly between the nation of Israel and God. The role of the individual was minimized. The priests and prophets did not teach on their own authority. Though the word disciple is not used in reference to this relationship per se, it is the *de facto* way that these leaders related to their followers. These followers would often take on the same ministry emphasis and embody the same message that their leader did. As is the case with Elisha and Elijah, the disciple had just as prominent a ministry as the leader. This in no way undermined the priority of their relationship with God. God was always given the central place but it could be said that these human discipleships were established by God to bring Israel into a closer walk with Himself.

The connection for believers today is clearly that our lives need to reflect the life Jesus lived. Even though "WWJD" became completely commercialized, the seed of the idea is valid: our individual and corporate actions and reactions should resemble that of Jesus. If those who profess to follow Jesus did nothing more than this, the church would reflect more clearly what we aspire to be.

USE IN JUDAISM

In rabbinic Judaism, the disciple is concerned with the entire written and spoken traditions, with particular emphasis given to their respective rabbi's interpretation of these traditions. The disciple subordinates himself to his rabbi with a deep commitment. In a sense, he "belongs" to his teacher. It is through the rabbi that the disciple can gain understanding of the scriptures, which in turn leads to deeper grasp of the character and ways of God. It is the rabbi's knowledge that gives him direct access to the scriptures, facilitating right hearing and right understanding. Listening to the scriptures without the guidance of a rabbi was to be avoided at all costs. The student was to evaluate the rabbi's teaching in light of the Torah to discover God's will, but the rabbi still functioned in the role of mediator between the Torah and his pupils.

There are important implications of the meaning of the term disciple within the context of Judaism in the time of Christ. First, the implications of what it meant to be a disciple depended on whom the disciple was following. Different teachers seemed to have unique expectations of their followers. Jesus' followers seem to be similar to disciples of other teachers of the time. However, Jesus radicalized the term in emphasizing that being a disciple was not a theoretical undertaking but a practical task of loving God and others, and doing God's work in the world. The end goal of Jesus' disciples was not to be a master teacher but rather a servant of all.

Further, this rabbinic context provides a rich background for many favourite passages about the ministry of Jesus. Jesus calls all who are weary and heavy laden to take His yoke (i.e. teachings and priorities) upon them and *learn from* Him (Mt. 11:29). As Christ's "sheep," His followers know His voice and *listen to Him* (Jn. 10:3, 16). The prophet Isaiah addresses the same idea in the proclamation that God has given Him "an ear to listen, as *one being instructed*" (Isa. 50: 4) and that "...He (the LORD) will teach us His ways so that we may walk in His paths" (Isa. 2:3).

The concept of "being a disciple" reaches its fullest understanding in the New Testament. Surprisingly, the plural form of the word disciple is the norm. The instances where the singular is used typically is in reference to particular people. It can be concluded that individual disciples are to be seen in the context of the community of disciples.

The term *disciple* in the New Testament could refer to a variety of groups. The disciples of Jesus not only included the twelve but also a larger group who were sympathetic to His teaching and were dedicated to Him in varying degrees. Those who were present throughout much of Jesus' earthly ministry could be placed into one of two groups. First, there were those normally thought of as disciples. This group was composed of the twelve and the larger group of followers (Lk. 6:13), who had a commitment to Jesus in some way. A second group, commonly described as the "crowds" or "multitudes," are occasionally referred to as disciples also (Jn. 6). This group was comprised of curious people who were not yet attached to Jesus in any serious way. Although they were said to follow Christ (Mt. 4:25), they only followed in a physical sense without making a true commitment of devotion. An objective of Jesus' ministry, then was to make committed followers out of this group.

Each of the gospel writers uniquely nuances the term disciple. In the book of Matthew, the author demonstrates that the Christian life is to be seen as equivalent to actually being with Jesus, living daily as His disciple. Individual distinctions among disciples are related to function, not to standing before God

(Mt. 12:49-50; 28:19-20). In Mark, the disciple is to experience and then extend a message that the penalty of sin has been paid and that the power of sin has been broken for those who follow Jesus (Mk. 10:42-45). In Luke, the way of the disciple who truly follows Jesus will be costly, but the power of God can accomplish the impossible (Lk. 9:23; 18:27-28). In John, the disciple is to be characterized by a profound experience with the love of God, which extends outward in loving others. This encounter with love must yield a desire and willingness to obey the commands of God (Jn. 14:23). John specifically connects being a disciple with being someone who has come out of the sphere of darkness into the sphere of light (3:21). A common aspect of being a disciple in all of the gospels is the connection with faith (Mk. 16:16; Lk. 17:5) and in Jesus Himself (Mt. 18:6).

Central Dimensions of Discipleship

New Testament scholar Michael Wilkins is one the foremost authorities on the Greek term μαθητηζ (*mathetes* or disciple). In *Following the Master* (1992), Wilkins highlights three pivotal aspects of being a disciple of Jesus. First is affirming that Jesus is the Son of God. In Matthew 16:15, Jesus asks His disciples "who do you say I am?" Peter responds in saying that Jesus is "the Messiah, the son of the living God." Affirming that Jesus is God is clearly expressed since the beginnings of the church, particularly in the Nicene Creed, and is established as central to orthodox Christianity.

A second dimension of being a disciple of Jesus is that salvation is seen as coming from Jesus alone (Jn. 6:68), that He alone is the way, the truth, and the life (Jn. 14:6). Throughout the ages and especially within the current context, the notion of salvation being found in Christ alone is difficult. This emphasis is shown again in Acts 4:12 where the writer says that "there is salvation found in no one else, for there is no other name under heaven given among men where we might be saved." The scriptures and the church have been unflinching in the conviction that the gospel is a stumbling block and a scandal. Many thousands of Christians have and are continuing to lose their lives over the declaration that Jesus is the only way.

The final aspect of being a disciple is that we are called to deny ourselves and to follow Jesus daily (Lk. 9:23). In following Jesus we are called to "count the cost" and to recognize no area of our lives can be reserved from Him. While not directly using the word disciple, Paul affirmed the seriousness of following Christ and frequently referred to the need among Christ-followers to yield themselves to God in consecrated obedience (Rom. 8:13), a command that parallels Christ's call for the disciple to deny himself (Mk. 8:34).

The Journey to Become a True Disciple

When reading the gospels as a whole, the process of becoming a disciple could be seen as occurring in stages. These stages are not divinely established nor do they occur in the same order every time. However, there are consistent elements seen in the scriptures as Jesus expanded the notion of what it meant to follow Him.

Initially, the individual recognizes Jesus as the Messiah and takes the personal initiative to follow Him. As Jesus was beginning His ministry, Andrew recognized that Jesus was the Messiah and brought his bother, Peter, to Jesus (Jn. 1:35-42). As is the case today, not everyone saw Jesus the same way. People began to come to Jesus for many different reasons. Some recognized His messianic identity and began to follow Him in ways that were similar to the disciples of other teachers, such as John the

Baptist. Others, such as the rich young ruler, came to Jesus because they were curious and had questions they wanted Jesus to
address (Lk. 18:18-27).

A second stage involved Jesus' individual call to follow Him.
This stage occurred when Jesus shifted His public ministry to
Galilee following the arrest of John the Baptist, and as He began
preaching that the kingdom of God was near (Mt. 4:12-17; Mk.
1:14-16). Jesus' call was a call to personal commitment to Him.
It also involved joining Him in the announcement that the kingdom of God had arrived. The pattern of Jesus calling His followers stayed consistent: (1) while going about the countryside, Jesus
would recognize the specific people He would call; (2) He would
summon them; (3) those who responded to the call would follow
Him at once. This practice of summoning others to follow Him
was replicated in the lives of His disciples. By emphasizing this
method of Christ's followers developing other followers (i.e. mul-
tiplication), the church grew rapidly throughout its early history.

The third stage involved Jesus sifting His followers by emphasizing the true nature of His earthly ministry and the corre-
sponding expectations (Lk. 9:59-62; 14:26). Upon hearing what
was required, many of the disciples were no longer willing to
follow Him. A specific example of this is Jesus' caveat that only
those who "eat the flesh of the Son of Man and drink his blood"
will have eternal life (Jn. 6:53). Upon hearing this, John says
many of his disciples said, "This is a hard teaching! Who can
accept it?...From this time many of his disciples turned back
and no longer followed Him" (Jn. 6:60, 66). The fourth and final
stage came during the final weeks before Jesus' crucifixion. The
number of those remaining faithful to Jesus became fewer and
fewer. It was becoming increasingly clear that Jesus was indeed
a "stumbling block" and that following Him would require a

commitment of everything. His was not a religion of convenience. Rather, Jesus was resolute in His call for a commitment that put no person or thing before Him. With the twelve, Jesus re-emphasized the essentials of the kingdom of God and what would happen after He was crucified (Jn. 13-17).

While in His earthly ministry and after His ascension, Jesus emphasized the importance of the Holy Spirit to His disciples (Jn. 16:5-15). The Spirit's role in growing in holiness or sanctification cannot be overlooked. In II Thessalonians 2:13, we see the following: "God chose you to be saved through the sanctifying work of the Spirit and through belief in the truth." As the believer seeks to live out their Christian life, it is the Spirit that mediates the personal presence of Christ (Jn. 14:15-26). Paul describes this as our bodies being the temple of the Spirit (I Cor. 6:19). The Spirit has an active role in the believer's pursuit of holiness: the Spirit convicts of sin (Jn. 16:8), brings spiritual fruit (Gal. 5:22-23), and reveals truth (Jn. 14:17; 16:13). The Spirit illumines the full meaning of the new life in Christ (I Thess. 1:4-5), with the Spirit being particularly active in the application and illumination of scripture in the believer's life.

Counting the Cost of Following Jesus: II Timothy 2:1-7

II Timothy 2:1-7 makes a good case for what it means to follow Jesus. The metaphors that Paul draws on provide special insight into what it practically means to be a Christ-follower.

Paul's words in II Timothy 2:1-7 have special significance to me. Having been raised on a cotton farm, I have some understanding of what is involved in bringing a crop to harvest. Countless hours of tending the cotton plants are required to see a harvest realized. Weather challenges and machinery issues have to be reckoned with throughout the growing season. As a long-distance runner, I am also aware that discipline and an ability to suffer are necessary parts of achieving a personal best. Through the vivid imagery of the farmer and athlete, as well as that of the soldier, the passage under consideration provides rich imagery for the church.

The passage serves as a reality check for the follower of Christ. As Paul nears the end of his life, he minces no words in articulating what the faithful life is to be like. The only way the Christian will be able to remain faithful to the end is to first "be strong in the grace that is in Christ Jesus" (II Tim. 2:1). We are saved by the grace of God but we are powerfully strengthened in life, and for life, by God's grace. It is by this grace that we will be able and willing to endure the suffering and hardship that will be associated with following Jesus.

> *You then, my son, be strong in the grace that is in Christ Jesus. And the things you have heard me say in the presence of many witnesses entrust to reliable men who will also be qualified to teach others. Join with me in suffering, like a good soldier of Christ Jesus. No one serving as a soldier gets entangled in civilian affairs, but rather tries to please his commanding officer. Similarly, anyone who competes as an athlete does not receive the victor's crown except by competing according to the rules. The hardworking farmer should be the first to receive a share of the crops. Reflect on what I am saying, for the Lord will give you insight into all this.* (II Tim. 2:1-7)

GRACE: THE SOURCE IN THE DISCIPLE'S LIFE

The first section of Chapter Two draws a sharp focus on encouragement and exhortation with a special focus given to "being strong." The service of Timothy and all believers should be characterized by and centered upon grace and power if the church is going to be effective against all that it will face. Here, grace is more connected to the notion of power (2 Tim. 1:7-8) than the notion of unmerited favour. This power is then based on grace that is, in turn, based on Jesus Christ. The disciple's life begins with and continues in grace alone. In verse two, Paul combines the requirement of personal spiritual strength with the need to rightly and effectively communicate the gospel message. Paul tells Timothy to entrust the ministry in Ephesus to others as he leaves to be with Paul in Rome. It is essential that faithful men who are capable teachers be selected for this task. As the Ephesian church fights against heresy (II Tim. 2:17-19) and as people fall away (II Tim.1:15), the integrity of the gospel message must be kept preserved. Central virtues for these men are reliable character and their ability to teach effectively.

SUFFERING AS A SOLDIER

In verse three, one of the principal themes of the passage comes to the fore. The soldier is the first of three metaphors where the idea of suffering for the gospel is addressed in varying degrees. The centrality of suffering within the life of a faithful soldier is obvious. The soldier willingly sacrifices his own well-being for the sake of a greater cause. This metaphor provides a connection with one of the overarching themes of the letter, namely, joining Paul in suffering for the sake of the gospel (II Tim. 1:6-8).

Verse four highlights perseverance as an additional aspect of being a soldier. The soldier's service must be marked by loyalty and a willingness to go the distance. This stands in marked contrast with those who have deserted Paul. The use of a present participle communicates that the soldier is actively engaged on an assignment. The operative words in verse four are "entangle" and "please." The implication is that Timothy should let nothing distract him. By use of the phrase "no one," the verse refers to all who follow Jesus. Timothy must give himself completely to Jesus, his commanding officer, even to the point of suffering.

THE DISCIPLINED ATHLETE

The second metaphor, the athlete, is introduced in verse five. The athlete is willing to suffer in training as the Christian must be willing to suffer for godliness (1 Tim. 4:7). Again, the word "anyone" refers to all Christians who strive to live the faithful life. As with the soldier, wholehearted devotion, self-control, and determination will be needed to contend with the stresses that will be placed on the mind and body. In competing in accordance with the rules, a strict regime of self-denial is necessary in order to receive the crown, which is "imperishable" (1 Cor. 9:24-27). The reference to the imperishable crown introduces an eschatological component to this metaphor and will be continued in the following verse.

THE COMMITTED FARMER

The theme of suffering continues here with the third and final metaphor of the image of the "hardworking farmer" in II Timothy 1:6. This image ties in the notions of striving and struggling, two favorite themes of Paul (1 Tim. 4:10; 5:17). The work that goes into planting, tending to, and harvesting a crop involves commitment and strenuous toil. This is the strongest reference to eschatological reward of the three metaphors. The reward that can be expected then is due to diligence and active focus. Taken together, these three pictures convey a consistent theme of linking disciplined, on-going effort to obtaining a valuable and worthwhile goal. Paul wraps up this passage by assuring Timothy that God will give him the understanding to fully comprehend what Paul has said. The same grace that will be needed to endure the suffering, compete according to the rules, and do the hard work of producing a harvest will give Timothy understanding.

Disciple-making and University Students

From the onset, let me say that the making of a disciple of Jesus Christ in the context of higher education is not, in its essence, any different than the making of a disciple in Botswana, Bolivia, or Brownfield, Texas. In every instance, a recognition of Jesus as the Son of God, seeing salvation as only found in Him, and a commitment to deny one's self and follow Him are common and unchanging. However, each of these contexts, the university campus included, will have unique issues that will influence how this process unfolds. In this final section of this chapter, I would like to address a few areas that are unique in helping students follow Jesus. I have worked in university ministry for most of my professional life and have come to see again and again that many university students face distinctive challenges in their spiritual growth.

The call to follow Jesus and see salvation as found solely in Him is as difficult today as it has been throughout history. Each year, scores and scores of people are killed and abused around the world due to their commitment to Christ. North American university students may not be persecuted to this extent, but they find it increasingly challenging to accept Jesus as the exclusive means to a relationship with God. University students are children of the postmodern age where perspectivism and a rejection of universal, objective truth rule the cultural landscape. A first issue then, for effective Christian higher education, is to establish a confidence in the objective truths of Christian orthodoxy. A Christian university's approach to epistemology (how we come to know things are true) must include correctly balanced commitments to revelation, reason, and the empirical realm. In coming to a confident yet humble resolve that God's truth can be known and that it serves as a guide for life inside and outside the academy, a student will have a foundation for the complexities of the world as it unfolds.

A second facet of discipleship in higher education is the pastoral role of helping students become confident in their understanding of their place as a child of God. It has been said that the university years are a season of train wrecks. While this seems like a dire assessment, there is some truth in this description. The university years are a time of great transition and change. Students will make good and bad choices as they move from being teens to young adults, and as they grow in their understanding of faith and their increasing autonomy. Many students, Christians included, shoulder tremendous amounts of shame and guilt over transgressions they have committed or that have been committed against them. Helping students move through these experiences, not becoming dominated by a sense of shame but still calling them toward to the holy life Jesus asks of them, is a central task.

The metaphors of soldier, athlete, and farmer are of particular relevance for spiritual formation within the academy. The soldier and athlete must commit to a goal beyond themselves. In *Souls In Transition* (2009), Christian Smith relates that American young adults can be characterized by the mindset that subjective, personal, and autonomous experience is what motivates action. That is to say, his research highlights that young adults struggle to commit to priorities that impinge on their own desires. Committing to the point where there is a real cost (finances, autonomy, social status) is outside the norm and even seen as extremism. A central tenet of North American culture is that the individual must always be able to choose, and that commitments are binding only in so far as they continue to be desired by the individual. The soldier and athlete strive in pursuit of a goal at great personal expense, but a goal that extends well beyond them. This reflects the selfless life of Christ and the difficult but ultimately rewarding call to follow Jesus.

REFERENCES

Smith, C. (2009). *Souls in transition*. New York: Oxford Press.

Wilkins, M. J. (1992). *Following the Master*. Grand Rapids: Zondervan.

ROB RHEA

---

*Tim McCarthy, MA, is the Associate Director of Student Ministries
for Chapel. A graduate of Trinity Western University and ACTS
Seminaries, he has been coordinating TWU's daily chapel program
and mentoring student worship leaders and artists since 1997. He
has been a workshop presenter on various issues of worship leadership and design, and on the role of worship in the academy, in various local events, as well as at the Calvin Symposium on Christian
Worship at Calvin College in Grand Rapids, MI.*

chapter 5

THE ROLE OF FACULTY IN STUDENTS' SPIRITUAL FORMATION THROUGH WORSHIP & PRAYER

TIM MCCARTHY

Toward a Definition of Spiritual Formation

A BIBLICAL DEFINITION OF SPIRITUAL FORMATION IS rooted in the Christian meta-narrative that forms all of reality: the gospel. Hearing the gospel again for the first time is essential to understanding the role of the Christian community in shaping students for citizenship in God's kingdom.

According to the Bible, God created the universe, and made this particular planet as a special home for His personal revelation of Himself—what Robert Webber (2006) has called "a theatre for His glory" (P. 32). He created humanity in His image, to be His special representatives on earth (Gen. 1:26-27). Humanity was entrusted with the responsibility of nurturing the whole of creation to its full potential, as they lived in intimate fellowship and worked in creative collaboration with Him and with one another (Gen. 1:28). It was His plan that they, with Him, would bring all manner of social, agricultural, horticultural, technological, scientific, and artistic wonders out of the raw materials of the newly-formed creation—all of them infused with the presence, love, and truth of God, so that the whole earth would be full of His glory.

Tragically, Satan entered into this garden of vast potential and convinced humanity that they could accomplish the task of ruling creation *apart from* intimate fellowship with God—that departing from God's plan would make them supreme beings in their own right. Because of his deception, they disregarded the fact that the true potential of creation, including their own role in it, was inextricably linked to the life and presence of God. As Romans says, "although they knew God, they did not honor Him as God or give thanks to Him, but they became futile in their thinking, and their foolish hearts were darkened" (Rom. 1:21 ESV). Their sinful ambition put them at odds with everything around them. Knowing God became a source of death instead of life. Knowing one another was fearful, and their differences became divisive and destructive instead of complementary. Knowing themselves brought shame instead of wonder. Creation became their enemy instead of their home and workshop. Instead of being partners with a good, truthful, and loving God, they became slaves to sin and to Satan's deceitful influence and accusing voice. In the words of Paul, apart from God's intervention humanity suffers from "the futility of their minds" (Eph. 4:17b). Paul goes on to say:

> *They are darkened in their understanding, alienated from the life of God because of the ignorance that is in them, due to their hardness of heart. They have become callous and have given themselves up to sensuality, greedy to practice every kind of impurity.* (Eph. 4:18-19)

In this inherited state of sin, every effort humanity has made to nurture creation's potential is ruined in varying manners and degrees, so that the fruit of humanity's social, agricultural, technological, scientific, and artistic efforts have always included pain and destruction for themselves and for the whole creation.

With grace and mercy, God re-initiated His relationship with humanity in the theatre of history. This theme of fellowship and partnership with God can be traced through all the biblical narratives: God's promise to Noah, God's covenant with Abraham, and God's relationship with the nation of Israel through the Law, the Davidic dynasty, the Temple, and the prophets. In each moment of history, God instructed His chosen people in how they, in fellowship with Him, might bring full flourishing to their moment in history and to their space on earth. In spite of their repeated failure, He promised a day when all creation's hopes would be realized, setting the stage for His own appearance in history in the person of Jesus Christ.

Fulfilling all of God's promises for restoration, Jesus Christ is the "image of God" (Col. 1:15), the "exact representation of his being" (Heb. 1:3), who "learned obedience through suffering" (Heb. 5:8) and therefore perfectly displayed what it was like for a man to walk in perfect fellowship with God in time and space. Through Jesus' redemptive work on the cross, and by His victory over death, a way was made to re-establish the connection to God, the Life of creation, that had been severed by sin. Guilt, shame, death, and evil lost their grip on humanity.

Having ascended into His rightful place as supreme ruler over creation, Jesus sent His own presence, in the person of the Holy Spirit, to dwell in the lives of those who have turned away from their selfish god-complex. By faith in Jesus Christ, a "new creation" has begun (II Cor. 5:17); across history and across the world, new communities of humans have been re-created to once again "image" the creator within the corner of creation for which they are responsible to care. According to Colossians 3:10, people are now invited to "put on the new self, which is being renewed in knowledge *after the image of its creator*," and in Ephesians 4:24, to "put on the new self, *created after the likeness of God* in true righteousness and holiness." This full renewal of humanity's capacity to "image" God is what all of creation longs for, as declared in Romans:

> *For the creation waits with eager longing for the re-*
> *vealing of the sons of God....And not only the creation,*
> *but we ourselves, who have the firstfruits of the Spirit,*
> *groan inwardly as we wait eagerly for our adoption as*
> *sons, the redemption of our bodies. For in this hope we*
> *were saved.* (Rom. 8:19,23-24a)

As creation waits for the day when all sin will be eliminated and humanity is completely renewed, the people of God, in a growing, living, transforming communion with God and with one another, are to be God's representatives. They announce, with their testimony, their faithful stewardship, and their suffering even unto death, the possibility of reconciliation with God and of restoring the creation, one surrendered life, family, community, and nation at a time. Together, God's people look forward to the day envisioned by the apostle John, when the heavens and the earth are made new, and what is celebrated in Revelation will come to pass:

> *Worthy are you [Jesus, the Lamb on the throne], for*
> *you were slain, and by your blood you ransomed* peo-
> ple for God *from every tribe and language and people*
> *and nation, and you have made them* a kingdom and
> priests *to our God, and* they shall reign on the earth.
> (Rev. 5:9-10)

Christians anticipate a day when we reach our full potential as humans in perfect communion with God, and are released to nurture the new creation toward its infinite potential as a theatre of God's glory, for all eternity: "Behold, the dwelling place of God is with man. He will dwell with them, and they will be his people, and God himself will be with them as their God" (Rev. 21:3). In the new creation, all political systems, economic structures, creative artistry, human relationships, and physical realities will be perfectly infused with and nurtured by the life-giving presence of the Triune God, so that tears and mourning and crying and pain are banished forever!

In light of this good news story, spiritual formation can be defined this way: spiritual formation is the ongoing process whereby people increasingly represent God's holy character and supernatural power within their personal and corporate sphere of influence in creation. They do so as they become united with God, through Christ, by the Spirit, modeling their lives after the life and teachings of Jesus, in community with others. In this, they witness to the day that all creation longs for, when God makes all things new.

Methods of Spiritual Formation in the Lives of Students

Therefore, a large part of our task as mentors and educators is to help students catch a vision for who they could be in the mission of God, if they were to respond to God's invitation to be united with Him in relationship and purpose.

In a society where the most powerful religious forces are, as James K. A. Smith (2009) has argued in *Desiring the Kingdom* (93-129), the pre-cognitive "liturgies" of the mall, patriotism, and the secular university, it is imperative that Christian communities, both church and academy, provide a more adequate and intentional liturgy for life—practices that shape their members' approach to time, relationships, resources, entertainment, and the use of their body, and thus shape their capacity to be available to God's work in their lives. It is especially important to help them discover what Dallas Willard calls "the secret of the easy yoke" (1990, P. 5): the surprising discovery that what the world considers onerous—to be holy and righteous—is attainable to some degree when we place ourselves in the company of Jesus, especially through the personal and corporate spiritual disciplines. As we're told in II Peter 1:3 and 5, "Everything that goes into a life of pleasing God has been miraculously given to us by getting to know, personally and intimately, the One who invited us to God... So don't lose a minute in building on what you've been given" (MSG).

One of the essential ways in which a Christian university campus can impart this vision for life is by modeling it in its corporate rhythms. This is why practices such as a regular chapel service are so essential to remaining Christ-centred; in campus gatherings of worship, we take a moment to "cease striving" (Ps. 46:10, NAS), delighting in the Triune God as the relational model of community, as the source of all for which we study and work, as the Lord and Teacher of our corporate and personal lives, and as the One toward whom all our endeavors point: "For from him and through him and to him are all things. To him be the glory forever" (Rom. 11:36, ESV). Especially in difficult seasons, it is critical for the community to rest in the character of God, to remember the gospel and all that it frees us to do, and to remember that we are, first and foremost, a community in covenant with a loving, providential, and self-revealing God.

Gathering together to worship allows the academic community to affirm together the fact that the gospel was God's plan "to *unite all things in [Christ]*, things in heaven and things on earth" (Eph. 1:10). Corporate worship in the academy is an opportunity to be a *united community that treasures Christ above all*. When we worship together, we treasure *the glory of Christ* as He has been revealed in creation, throughout history, and especially in the gospel. We treasure *the way of Christ*—His life and teachings, death and resurrection, as they are revealed throughout Scripture. We treasure *the voice of Christ*, in the myriad of ways He speaks across our vocations. We treasure *the Body of Christ*, His hands and feet that live and pray for His will to be done on earth as it is in heaven. And we treasure *the creativity of Christ*—who in His incarnation modeled for us what beauty and holiness and justice look like with flesh and bones.

In the busyness of academic routines, it is often difficult for faculty to make campus worship a priority. Yet students are affected by the presence of their mentors and teachers in the worshiping community—they see that their mentors are not just teachers about God, but lovers of God. Chapel is also a special opportunity to connect with students on a different level, perhaps by following up a challenging chapel message or time of corporate worship with a brief but intentional conversation on the sidewalk or in the class that follows.

But this is not the only way faculty can contribute to their students' formation as lovers of God. Following are some of the ways we can model this unity in treasuring Christ above all in the academy, beyond chapel.

Christian teachers affirm that Jesus Christ is the source of all insight, and His presence is what makes all knowledge, insight, creativity, innovation, profit and fruitfulness truly enduring and satisfying. Through invocations, prayers and intercessions in the classroom environment, teachers can acknowledge this Lordship over whatever sphere of study is being considered, as well as over the triumphs and joys, anxieties and grief of the students who are present. Faculty must never underestimate the power of their Christ-treasuring prayers in modeling to students what it is like to live, work, and study in fellowship with Christ.

A model of Christ-treasuring living is displayed when faculty share the ways that they are being led into deeper communion with God through the good and bad circumstances of their own lives. While there are limits to what an instructor might share on a personal level, students need to see that passionate worship and devotion to Christ is forged in the furnace of living, and the testimony of their faculty can have an enduring impact in this regard.

Whether it is a formal part of a faculty's role or not, it is inevitable that at one time or another, a student will come to a faculty member for counsel—perhaps regarding course selection or the details of an assignment, but often for more personal issues as well: fear for a parents' marriage, shame about a poor decision, financial stress, grief, or serious doubts. This is a precious moment of trust and vulnerability that has tremendous potential if a faculty member is willing to steward that moment in dependence on the Holy Spirit. In these encounters, alongside of our life's wisdom or personal presence, the best thing we can do is connect students in a personal way with Jesus Christ. Praying with them, listening to God for them and with them, and offering the perspective of a seasoned life of faith can be tremendous gifts in their lives.

Students also need to see modeled for them an understanding that every task can be infused with the presence of Jesus. Christian academic communities are fond of saying, "Jesus is

Lord over all things," and "All truth is God's truth." But students want to see that these are more than distant intellectual propositions. They are wondering, "Is it possible to experience God's truth and Christ's Lordship as a personal, moment-by-moment experience that we model in our lifestyles, conversations, and relationships across our campus?" As faculty grow in their own spiritual journeys, they must also share, as the Lord gives them opportunity, the processes and resources by which the Holy Spirit continues to teach them how to practice the presence of Christ, so that students can also go further on that journey.

Students must see their teachers being transparent about their own struggles to be faithful to Christ as well. They need to know that living out God's purposes is not always easy. In those areas where a person is ashamed of his or her life in Christ, it is important to take some time for self-examination, and allow the Holy Spirit to restore a sense of communion with God. When worship and prayer have become peripheral to one's life as a teacher and researcher and mentor, it may be time to ask, "Have I lost touch of the depths of communion to which Jesus invites me, even in, or perhaps especially in, those areas of my life?" While one's expression of that communion with Christ is going to be different from person to person, students need to see that there are many ways to commune with God, and that the propositions, "All truth is God's truth" and "Jesus is Lord of all" are living realities in their mentors' lives.

Students even pay attention to the ways in which faculty participate in and speak about the church. They need to see their professors and mentors meaningfully engaged with the mission of God in a local church. In many cases, they will be worshiping beside their teachers in local churches. Sometimes they will hear about an instructor's insights or critiques regarding the church in a lecture or conversation. In many cases, students make critical choices about the tradition in which they will or will not worship based on the model or teaching of their professors and mentors. They are observing the way in which their mentors are participating with the Body of Christ in the world, and they will shape their own engagement, at least in part, by what they see.

In a society where more and more families are dysfunctional, many students are also very hungry to experience the presence of Christ in a family. Some of them have never prayed with their family. Some of them have never experienced sincere, life-honouring fellowship around a table. While faculty must always be aware of appropriate boundaries, practicing God's hospitality becomes a powerful encounter with the presence of Christ for both student and host faculty.

In all of these ways, faculty contribute to a student's "total immersion" experience, in which God's presence permeates the entire community in its fellowship, labour, language, and practices. God invites anyone who teaches or mentors students in any capacity to take seriously Christ's command to abide in Him, personally and as a university community. He dares all to claim His promise that such abiding is the true source of fruitfulness in every realm of human endeavor. And He calls faculty and staff in the Christian community to step up to the role in which students have already placed them, as living, breathing examples of the transforming power of the gospel and of life in the Spirit. Especially in a community that proclaims the Lordship of Christ over all things, those who lead and teach must not believe or model that communion with Christ is a purely private thing, never to be observed by students.

However, the secret life of prayer is also essential to the Christian faculty's role. While a remarkable wealth of insight and wisdom is present among the Christian faculty and staff, the truth is that each one is, at most, a planter or a waterer (1 Cor. 3:7); it is God who gives the increase. This ministry of praying God's kingdom into the lives of students ought to be seen as essential to the vocation of Christian teacher—a profound trust that faculty and mentors steward as individuals, as departments, and as a university. At what other university will a student be not only taught, but held up in prayer to the Teacher of all teachers, who alone turns teaching into transformational learning?

A common objection to this vision of faculty's role in students' spiritual formation is simply that of margin and boundaries. In today's academically competitive and economically strapped environment, the burden that is placed on faculty and other staff mentors can be overwhelming. It can seem easier to delegate the role of spiritual mentor to others in the community, and continue on with one's institutional or instructional tasks. Christian institutions must make honest assessment of their underlying systems to determine whether the very rhythms and goals of the university may undermine the institution's ability to be fully present to the formational needs of the students. Institutions must take responsibility for creating an environment that is conducive to developing rich, healthy relationships between students and faculty where knowledge, wisdom, love, concern, and rest can be given and received.

In closing, consider again the gospel-rooted definition of spiritual formation: spiritual formation is the ongoing process by which people increasingly represent God's holy character and supernatural power within their personal and corporate sphere of influence. This occurs as we become united with God, through Christ, by the Spirit, modeling our lives after the life and teachings of Jesus, in community with others. Jesus' incredible promise in John speaks of this intimate fellowship in this way: "Whoever has my commandments and keeps them, he is the one who loves me. He who loves me will be loved by my Father, and I will love him and manifest myself to him… If anyone loves me, he will keep my word, and we will come to him and make our home with him" (Jn. 14:21,23). If students could begin to taste the wonder of that verse under their teachers' influence, how fruitful could they be as they are sent out into the world's greatest opportunities and deepest needs?

Teachers and mentors, embrace your role as models of a life lived in communion with God. Then, your little realm in God's kingdom can be increasingly filled with the knowledge of the glory of the Lord. It is appropriate to close with the words of the apostle Paul to the Corinthians:

> *And we all, who with unveiled face, beholding the glory of the Lord, are being transformed into the same image from one degree of glory to another. For this comes from the Lord who is the Spirit… For God, who said, "Let light shine out of darkness," has shone in our hearts to give us the knowledge of the glory of God in the face of Jesus Christ. But we have this treasure in jars of clay to show that the surpassing power belongs to God and not to us.* (II Cor. 3:18, 4:6-7)

May our broken and limited lives more fully reflect the glory and power of God, as we are united in treasuring Christ above all.

REFERENCES

Smith, J. K. A. (2009). *Desiring the kingdom*. Grand Rapids, MI: Baker Academic.

Webber, R. E. (2006). *The divine embrace: recovering the passionate spiritual life*. Grand Rapids, MI: Baker Books.

Willard, D. (1990). *The spirit of the disciplines*. San Francisco: HarperOne.

David Squires, Ph.D., is Dean of the School of the Arts, Media and Culture at Trinity Western University. A long-time university professor, mentor, and composer, he has also served as a worship pastor for several churches across Canada. His extensive catalogues of compositions range from chamber music to large ensemble, and his musicians range from amateurs and students to church groups and professional ensembles.

chapter 6

Spiritual Formation, The Imago Dei & Nurturing Creativity

DAVID SQUIRES

IN THE FIRST CLASS OF MY COURSE IN WORSHIP Foundations, I begin by scrawling on the whiteboard an equation: *worship ≠ music*

This is usually fairly provocative, especially for the guitar players in the crowd who thought they were in for an easy three credits! *"Surely the foundations of worship are: the key of D, three chords to accompany a song, a high tenor voice to lead with, and the ability to pray passionately with your eyes closed and your arms raised."* Many Christians equate music and worship, particularly in our contemporary church where music seems to dominate the non-preaching portions of what we call worship services. Our students, like us, have heard sermons on worship being a lifestyle—worship is 24/7, not just Sunday morning—but somehow it hasn't yet taken hold fully, and they are often confused about it.

Once I have students' attention with this startling equation, we start digging into scripture to explore the richness of biblical worship theology and practice, and then move into the church's history to explore how believers have inculturated a theology of worship variously through different ages. One of our wonderful guides in this journey of discovery is David Peterson, whose book *Engaging with God* (1992) proceeds from the thesis that "true worship is an engagement with [God], on the terms that he proposes, and in the way that he alone makes possible" (P.20). The last two of those three key points provide much grist for the mill: that worship is on God's terms, not according to our definitions and design; and that He alone makes it possible, we don't simply invite Him to show up in our meetings. But it is the first part of the sentence that deserves attention in today's discussion: that worship is engagement with God. This thesis captivates many students of worship, as they reflect on what this means for all of life.

Engaging with God is something we can understand as constant, as apart from the narrow connection with music. This is the relational emphasis of so much of scripture. We are thunderstruck with the sheer tragedy of Jesus' words on the cross, "My God, why have you forsaken me" (Mt. 27:46 NIV), and then later lifted to the heights with His words to the disciples, "Surely, I am with you always" (Mt. 28:20). Samuel Balentine, in his book *The Torah's Vision of Worship* (1999), relates this engagement of God with His people to the establishment of their identity. Balentine maintains that the Torah calls the community of faith to its most distinctive way of being the people of God in this world. It does so by affirming, among other things, that worship is a means of honouring, sustaining, and restoring God's creational design for the world; and that worship is at the heart of community building and world construction. The Torah, then, links God's purposes in worship with His purposes in the identity of the people of God.

Teaching students about worship, therefore, is really leading them to explore and deepen their identity as the people of
God. And here is where I make a link which takes me away
from worship *per se*, and into the *Imago Dei*, creativity, teaching or nurturing creativity, and how all this relates to spiritual
formation.

I think that a great part of spiritual formation is really about
identity, specifically one's identity as bearer of the *Imago Dei*.
I'll take the liberty of quoting a definition of spiritual formation used by my colleague Tim McCarthy. Note the emphasis
on identity:

> *Spiritual formation is the ongoing process whereby
> people increasingly represent God's holy character and
> supernatural power within their personal and cor-
> porate sphere of influence in creation. They do so as
> they become united with God, through Christ, by the
> Spirit, modeling their lives after the life and teachings
> of Jesus, in community with others.*[1]

Spiritual formation has much to do with identity: our identity
as children of God, our identity with Christ, and our identity
as those who are made in God's image. In his introduction,
Rob Rhea laid out the three-part model used in TWU's Student
Ministries: the inward life, the upward life, and the outward life.
In many ways we can see those emphases in the structure of
these presentations in this retreat. We can also hear their echoes
in words like *human agency*, *divine agency*, and *community*. As

1. see Chapter 5.

we explore spiritual formation in the student's life, and equally in our own, identity becomes entwined with relationship. I am made in the image of God, and so are you.

I'll make reference to Tim McCarthy again and his wonderful exploration of an alternate reality, one in which Eve simply said to the serpent, "Uh, no…I'll pass on that, thank you":

> *Humanity was entrusted with the responsibility of nurturing the whole of creation to its full potential, as they lived in intimate fellowship and worked in creative collaboration with Him and with one another (Gen. 1:28). It was His plan that they, with Him, would bring all manner of social, agricultural, horticultural, technological, scientific, and artistic wonders out of the raw materials of the newly-formed creation—all of them infused with the presence, love, and truth of God, so that the whole earth would be full of His glory.[2]*

So now, armed with identity and relationship as important elements of spiritual formation, I want to switch gears to my part in the curriculum of the Music Department, mentoring student composers as they explore their identity as creative artists.

In my course objectives I am intentional about exploring the implications of *Imago Dei* for the student composer. I speak of "developing the student's understanding of the integration of the compositional gift with the Christian faith, exploring the relationship between God the Creator and the composer as a creator." I'm not alone in this: TWU's School of the Arts, Media and Culture is marked in all of its departments by the teach-

2. see Chapter 5.

ing and nurturing of creativity, within the context of the image we all bear of a Creator God. For me, this is a paradigm which elevates my understanding of artistic creation way beyond the realm of entertainment, beyond the realm of the optional value-added component to the human life. No, we create because we are made in the image of a Creator God. We create because we must. It is who we are as human beings. When we create something, when we dream up and then execute something which did not exist moments before, we are like Him. And it is this paradigm which is revolutionary to a student's sense of self, his or her identity as a child of God. In the fact of our creativity we have the union of human agency and divine agency.

Contemporary Scottish composer James MacMillan has taught me much about this intersection of the human and the divine, notably in his reflections on Mary as a model for creative artists and, indeed, all Christians. He says:

> *There is something in the instinct of an artist or a composer, or any creative person, or any Christian for that matter, which is inexorably drawn to the idea of Mary's vesselship—the notion of making oneself as a channel for the divine will. This is not, of course, to negate the individual's human will. The incarnation came about through Mary's free and rational acceptance of God's plan for her. Similarly an artist or composer who thinks in real and meaningful terms of a divine inspiration would be mistaken in underestimating the full and active participation of all one's human faculties. It is through the interaction of all that makes us human—our intellect, our intelligence, our emotion and our physicality, our universal experience of joy and*

> *despair, our flesh and blood—with the breath of God*
> *which brings forth creative fruit.* (MacMillan, 2003, PP.
> 45-46)

So what does this have to do with spiritual formation? For me, these things become the curriculum behind the curriculum. And there are times when they actually take first place, and I am very intentional with students. I often tell students that, in the course of analyzing the works of others, and teaching them techniques for manipulating notes, rhythms, instrumental colours, and formal structures, I am really far *less* concerned that they finish the course having written something astonishingly beautiful or significant. I am far *more* concerned that they discover their compositional *voice* and are able to use that voice with authenticity and commitment, in a deep relationship with God their creator, and with the community in which they find themselves. Their bodies and their art, a living sacrifice, is their spiritual worship (Rom. 12:1)—not a metaphor, but a worship reality. And now we've come back around the circle to worship again.

This was not really my own experience in undergraduate or graduate school. Not one of the fine composers who were my composition teachers was concerned for my inner life. Not one in three leading Canadian and American universities spoke to my formation as a person. They were busy looking at my music and couldn't see my heart. This is a mistake I can't afford to make with my students.

I marvel at the wonder of God's gift of creativity. The one who made all things out of His imagination, who spoke things into being from nothing—things which had not even been thought before—has given us, His creatures, the ability to make things! We do not make things from nothing as He did, but create we do, nevertheless. When I take up the elements of time and vibrations, of wood or metal objects, of human breath or bodily movement, when I apply my imagination to these things, when I think and dream a piece of music into being—this is a wonder beyond me. Simply put, the music which comes out was not there a few moments before. It appears on the stage of the world, a newborn thing for all to see, the product of an imagination given the great gift of the kind of power that God Himself has. This is a mystery indeed!

Many thinkers have taken a stab at this kind of mystery. Jacques Attali said that music "is a way of perceiving the world" (*Noise*, 1985, P. 4). In *Music: A Very Short Introduction*, Nicholas Cook suggests that music may be "a way of constructing a reality (a world)" (1998, P. 75). Yet this world, freshly created by a composer or musician, is not a robust thing like the worlds our God has created. It is fraught with fragility. Here I want to turn to another Scot, a theologian whose writings on Celtic spirituality have been part of my spiritual formation. Noel Dermot O'Donoghue wrote, in his book *The Angels Keep Their Ancient Places* (2001):

> *What I began to see was that certainty and the desire for absolutes understood absolutely were, on the whole, bad for human beings, and that we have in us another faculty by which truth can be received gently and tentatively as an ongoing relationship and courtship. This, I saw, is precious, but it is totally destroyed if I grasp it tightly and fiercely as a possession held fast against all that would question or add to it. This faculty or power I came to call the faculty of intimation.* (P. 66)

Let me dig into the rich soil of this paragraph a bit, and see how it ultimately affects my approach to spiritual formation in the students with whom I journey. Music doesn't exist in the realm of the absolute; it is much more related, as is art, to the realm of intimation. The composer is not a scientist, but a philosopher — asking questions, challenging assumptions, presenting ideas which are much more ephemeral and intangible than the logic centre of our being tends to like to think about. Creativity deals in this kind of activity — asking questions, postulating realities.

God spoke, and because of His omnipotence, His words and ideas became actual and real. We speak creatively, and though we are not omnipotent as God, nonetheless our ideas go forth with enough power to move others to consider the reality which we intimate. We speak possibilities, asking the question: "could it be?" The listener then joins us in pondering that potentiality. This is how meaning resides in the creative act. The imagination of the artist first asks the question, "could it be?" of him or herself. Then the question is laid out for the other, who joins in (or not) to become part of the journey.

All of this does not mean that the question is a concrete one, as science's questions so often are. And the means of expressing the question are not like the concrete speech and rational inquiry of the humanities. They are spoken in harmonies, melodies, instrumental colours, and rhythmic patterns. This is not the world of the concrete and the absolute.

This kind of meaning, both expressed and received, joined with and journeyed alongside, must be (in O'Donoghue's words again) "received gently and tentatively as an ongoing relationship and courtship." If we come to music, either as composer, performer, or receiver, hoping to "grasp it tightly or fiercely as a possession," with our understanding of its meanings "held fast against all that would question or add to it," then we will surely destroy it. It is too fragile for that kind of rough treatment. The quest for domination which is so much a part of our human existence will undo our art. Making art is like making love — it must be filled with tenderness, respect, and self-sacrifice.

Music may be a way of perceiving the world; it may be a way of constructing a world; it may reflect reality; it may depict or signify things or emotions. Whatever music means, I believe we must approach it with humility and gentleness among other things. Our former dean, Linda Schwartz, used this expression in a course syllabus in Music theory and analysis: "...*to explore the past (and present) charitably, critically, and reflectively.*" For the reality of the world the composer has created or reflected is a fragile and tentative one. It is not the robust created world of our Almighty God, but the tentative and vulnerable world of the creature — the one made in the *Imago Dei* — a world pregnant with possibilities yet open to misunderstanding.

Finally, I think that creativity and spiritual formation intersect in this — they are both vulnerable and fragile. They both exist in a realm which Simon Critchley refers to in his *Continental Philosophy: A Very Short Introduction* (2001), as the gap between knowledge and wisdom. He has said that "We live with — and within — a gap between knowledge and wisdom. It is time philosophers, and everyone else, started to try and think about that gap" (p. 122).

I find myself playing in that gap constantly, both in terms of my own spiritual formation, and my life as a creative creature made in the image of my Creator God. I invite my students into the gap with me, not simply to explore but to try to test the width of the gap, and to try to close it ever so humbly and tentatively, boldly and bravely. In this we explore together issues like identity, relationship, and community, and along the way we often make some pretty good art too!

REFERENCES

Attali, J. (1985). *Noise*. Minnesota, MN: University of Minnesota
Press.

Balentine, S. (1999). *The Torah's vision of worship*. Minneapolis:
Fortress Press.

Cook, N. (1998). *Music: A very short introduction*. Oxford: Oxford
University Press.

Critchley, S. (2001). *Continental philosophy: A very short
introduction* Oxford: Oxford University Press.

MacMillan, J. (2003). God, theology, and music. In Stephen
Darlington and Alan Kreider (eds.). *Composing music for
worship* (pp.). Norwich: Canterbury Press.

O'Donoghue, N. D. (2001). *The angels keep their ancient places*.
Edinburgh: T&T Clark.

Peterson, D. (1992). *Engaging with God*. Downers Grove, IL:
InterVarsity Press.

Lynn R. Szabo, Associate Professor of American Literature and Creative Writing in the English Department at Trinity Western University, is a scholar of the poet, mystic, and peace activist Thomas Merton, an emerging, significant figure in twentieth century literary studies. She has authored numerous articles on his poetics and is the editor of In the Dark Before Dawn: New Selected Poems of Thomas Merton *(2005); she has also recently co-edited* Through a Glass Darkly: Suffering, The Sacred and The Sublime in Literature and Theory *(2010). Lynn treasures her Christian heritage and seeks spiritual pathways which enable contemplation, peace, solitude, and their attendant discoveries in the life of the university teacher and researcher.*

Love & The Search for God

LYNN R. SZABO

LOVE & THE SEARCH FOR GOD

My Lord God
I have no idea where I am going.
I do not see the road ahead of me.
I cannot know for certain where it will end.
Nor do I really know myself, and the fact that I think I am
following your will does not mean that I am actually doing so.
But I believe that my desire to please you does in fact please you.
And I hope that I have that desire in all that I am doing.
I hope that I will never do anything apart from that desire.
And I know that if I do this you will lead me by the right road
though I may know nothing about it.
Therefore will I trust you always though I may seem to be lost
and in the shadow of death.
I will not fear, for you are ever with me, and you will never leave
me to face my perils alone.

- Thomas Merton (1958, P. 79)

In this exquisite prayer, Thomas Merton gives words to the lived experience of the human search for God and the desire for His will. The joy of every believer is that in this search, Christianity offers the only story of God taking on human form in Christ's redemptive work; the bodily resurrection of Christ to life eternal offered to all who believe; the comfort and teaching of the Holy Spirit for all who wish to know Christ in this life and the Scriptures that teach us how we can grow spiritually in response to the love of God in our lives. In these ways, Christian spirituality creates a vitality and dynamic life in those who embrace it. Jeremiah tells us that when we search for God with all our heart, we will find Him and we will be found of Him (Jer. 29:13-14). This search is the essence of the Christian's life. It promises intimacy with God that culminates in the personhood of Jesus Christ—the Incarnation that lives in every impulse in the believer toward receiving God's love: "We love because He first loved us" (1 Jn. 4:19 NRSV).

In his fine exploration of the intentionality of this love, *Reaching Out: The Three Movements of the Spiritual Life*, Henri Nouwen (1998) describes an instructive path for the one who is seeking to find and love God. First, we reach out to our innermost self. In doing so by the quiet and private practice of self-examination, we find that the "tension of loneliness" is exchanged for a listening solitude in which we gain self-knowledge that is a preparation for the next stages of spiritual development. Socrates posited that "the unexamined life is not worth living." Scripture goes much farther. It proclaims that in the meditations of the heart the perfect law of the Lord converts the soul, making wise the simple (Ps. 19:7-14). The delights of this conversion are "sweeter than the honeycomb" or in present-day metaphor, indulge a sweetness that goes beyond any possible eye or ear candy that can be offered to us as pleasure or instruction.

In order to be prepared for such profound experience, we must first understand our unique and individual personhood and its possibilities for relation to God—how it bears the *Imago Dei* in God's specific creation of each of us: "My substance was not hid from You, when I was made in secret… In your book were written all the days that were formed for me, when none of them as yet existed" (Ps. 139:15-16). In this recollection of the self, as Jonathan Edwards explains, we are led to our rest in the "fundamental beauty" of God's particular love for us and in the righteousness of Christ that we bear, as Paul describes in 2 Corinthians 5:21: "For our sake he made him to be sin who knew no sin, so that in him we might become the righteousness of God."

It follows therefore, that the authentically-educated Christian person is one who has sought self-knowledge in and beyond the paradigms of the various disciplines that attempt to point one on the path to self-understanding and wisdom within the academic environment. In such discipline, we learn to love in ourselves what God has placed in our hearts to love, His image in us, the love of our own particular humanity as it has been created to respond individually to God's love for us. The self-love that is discovered in informed self-examination is that which Jesus referred to when He taught us the new commandment: "Love your neighbour as yourself" (Lev. 19:18).

The second aspect of our ongoing conversion of the heart toward God takes place in our response to the human community. It is here where we confront the "tension of hostility" (Nouwen, 1998) being converted to hospitality. Our ability to act benevolently is the root of our choice to love our neighbours by finding happiness in their good. When they are happy, our own happiness derives from it, as does God's in our happiness. This extends into every aspect of our daily life in Christ, particularized as Jesus describes it in the essential details of daily life: when you have given food and drink to others who are thirsty and hungry, when you have visited the sick and the imprisoned, when you have clothed the naked, you have done it unto Him (Mt. 25:40). In our university environment, this includes offering life-giving meditation on the laws of God to the individual and community, spiritual guidance to all who seek, God-informed art and science to the scholar and student. Such is completely contrary to an environment of entertainment, pleasure-seeking, self-indulgence, and facile accomplishment. It requires careful thought about how to intentionally love oneself and one's neighbour.

This is a call for a personal mission statement supported and nourished by the community in which it is to be lived out. Such a "Rule of Life," as it was called by the early Christians, was established as they sought to survive and flourish in a world which threatened to extinguish all that they held dear, one with many similarities to the world we now live in. St. Benedict is most well-known for his master-plan for spiritual formation that called for the balance of work, prayer, and study in the daily routine. In our socially-driven culture, this sounds archaic but when one enters academic life, one cannot be successful without taking great heed to this guidance. The Apostle Paul has laid it out very clearly in Ephesians 5:14-19, where wisdom is the outcome of spiritual formation that is focused on "redeeming our time." The possibilities for establishing this life are myriad: retreats, quiet days, daily chapel worship, personal study and intellectual formation, works of mercy, environmental responsibility, personal wellness, hospitality, and the desire for holiness. Indeed, they encompass every aspect of life and offer rewards beyond any imagined or experienced joys and what we call "fun," when they are engaged with the intention of showing our love to Christ in God. They are transformed from duties and commitments to precious acts of love when seen in this light.

The third aspect of spiritual formation that Nouwen explains is our movement toward the love of God and life in His intimate presence through Christ's redemptive work. It is in this pursuit that we live in the "tension of our illusions" being converted to prayer (Nouwen, 1998). We move from rejoicing in ourselves and others to a limitless rejoicing in God. In some ways, this approach turns things on their heads in terms of how we might have understood the Christ-life as one that begins with conversion and works outwards from there. Perhaps this gives us an alternative in that Nouwen's approach ennobles the education of the whole person as the groundwork for our becoming fully conscious of the potential to become Christlike; recollecting the image of God within each human person whereby education promotes the maturation of practises and beliefs that might have been spawned in the early stages of their spiritual formation, however nascent, even as unformed as that portrayed in Paul's anthropology of personhood and culture in Romans 1.

Parker Palmer, a leading Protestant writer on spiritual formation and academic education, can be recommended as one of Christianity's finest teachers on the spiritual life in the secular world. His mentorship was highly influenced by the writings of Thomas Merton, but he has rationalized them for a Protestant readership, desiring to discover some of the strengths of traditional Catholic spiritual and intellectual formation—the strongest tradition in Christianity in this regard. Merton explained in *No Man is an Island* (1978) that a person of spiritual and intellectual intention "works in an atmosphere of prayer, that is to say, that person is an engaged presence," proposing every detail of life as a gift of worship to God. Palmer applies this to the classroom, claiming that the teacher is one whose "soul is the primary resource in education." The student becomes the reciprocal agent in such "teachable moments." In *The Courage to Teach* (1997) and *To Know As We Are Known* (1993), Palmer observes this in Jesus' pedagogy as teacher of His disciples, followers and even His enemies. The potential of such a community of teachers and learners seeking to be disciples of Christ is awe-inspiring and joy-commanding.

My most precious hope for Trinity Western University is that we engage, at the deepest levels of intentionality, the spiritual formation which we understand as the ground and process of being transformed, by the Holy Spirit, through Christ, into His image and likeness. The educational enterprise in this environment will awaken in all of us the innate intuitive capacity of students to develop an awareness of their intrinsic ability to apprehend the mystery and reality of their own being. In such recognition, spiritual realities can be embraced by learning that is both cognitive and intuitive, rational and incarnational, full of inner and outer knowledge and wisdom, and most importantly, a preparation for the highest calling to love God. In this paradigm, we study all of life in order to love—ourselves, our neighbours, and God, with our whole hearts, minds, and souls. If we do so, we will create an authentic awareness in our community of the unique and luxurious invitation by which God is calling us to an ever-increasing intimate, loving life of participation in His Divine Nature and Incarnation.

REFERENCES

Merton, T. (1978). *No man is an island*. New York: Harcourt, Brace & Company.

Merton, T. (1958). *Thoughts in solitude*. New York: Farrar, Straus, Giroux.

Nouwen, H. (1986). *Reaching out: The three movements of the spiritual life*. New York: Doubleday.

Palmer, P. (1997). *The courage to teach: Exploring the inner landscape of a teacher's life*. San Francisco (CA).

Palmer, P. (1993). *To know as we are known: Education as a spiritual journey*. New York: HarperCollins.

Further Reading

RESOURCES WRITTEN IN A MORE POPULAR STYLE

Brother Lawrence. (2005). *The practice of the presence of God and spiritual maxims*. New Kensington, PA: Whitaker House.

Brother Lawrence lived in France from 1611-1691 and wrote this classic memoir of his devotional life while serving in a monastic order.

—

Bonhoeffer, D. (1954). *Life together*. New York: Harper & Rowe.

Imprisoned and later martyred in Germany for his faith during World War II, Dietrich Bonhoeffer wrote this manual, during his incarceration, to guide the building of Christian community.

—

Bunyan, J. (2000). *The pilgrim's progress in modern english*. Lafayette, IN: Sovereign Grace.

This is a newer, and more readable edition of Bunyan's classic work originally written in 1678 as a guide to the Christian journey.

—

Coleman, R. E. (1993). *The master plan of evangelism.* Tarrytown, NY: Revel.

Though the title may not reflect this, Coleman's book is a classic about how Jesus discipled the twelve toward spiritual maturity.

—

Foster, R. (1988). *Celebration of discipline: The path to spiritual growth.* San Francisco: Harper.

Foster's book is a classic on spiritual disciplines that lead to spiritual growth. Foster explores twelve disciplines divided into three categories: inward disciplines, outward disciplines, and corporate disciplines.

—

Lewis, C.S. (1973). *The great divorce.* New York: Harper.

In Lewis' "imaginative supposal," even in hell, lost souls remain free to accept God's grace, and yet do not. The story chronicles the responses of a bus load of hell's inhabitants to an imaginary tour of heaven. It offers a window into the fallen human psyche, with its pettiness, vanity and capacity for self-deception, where some humans keep finding creative ways to say no to God's yes for them in Christ.

—

Imbach, J. (1998). *The river within: Loving God, living passionately.* Colorado Springs: NavPress.

Imbach explores the ways in which our passion and longings

can lead us to embrace God more fully and deepen our spiritual lives.

—

Pettit, P. (2008). *Foundations of spiritual formation: A community approach to becoming like Christ.* Grand Rapids: Kregel.

This book is a compilation of eleven essays on a biblical basis for formation as well as several dimensions of formation such as the soul, character, and leadership. Most of the contributors are connected to Dallas Theological Seminary in some way.

—

Willard, D. (2002). *Renovation of the heart: Putting on the character of Christ.* Colorado Springs: NavPress.

Dallas Willard is one of the most prolific current authors on moral/spiritual formation today. In this work, he defines spiritual formation and looks at the process of formation by beginning with a focus on the renewing of the mind and moving outward to the whole person through concentric levels of transformation.

MORE CHALLENGING SUGGESTIONS

Chan, S. (1998). *Spiritual theology: A systematic study of the Christian life.* Downers Grove, IL: InterVarsity.

Spiritual theology is a more formal title for the study of the renewed life as one seeks to follow Christ. Chan brings a breadth of perspectives (theology, literature, sociology, etc.) to better understand growth in Christ.

—

Wilkins, M. J. (1992). *Following the master: Discipleship in the steps of Jesus.* Grand Rapids: Zondervan.

This is a very thorough biblical exploration of the term "disciple." Though a bit technical at times, it brings to light all of the richness of this central biblical term.